"IS THERE ANYTHING I CAN DO?"

"IS THERE ANYTHING I CAN DO?"

Helping a Friend When Times Are Tough

Sol Gordon

Delacorte **Press**

Published by
Delacorte Press
Bantam Doubleday Dell Publishing Group, Inc.
1540 Broadway
New York, New York 10036

Library of Congress Cataloging in Publication Data
Gordon, Sol, 1923–
Is there anything I can do? / Sol Gordon.
p.   cm.
Includes bibliographical references.
ISBN 0-385-29900-1
1. Friendship.   2. Helping behavior.   I. Title.
BF575.F66G67   1994
158'.25—dc20   93-44315 CIP

Designed by Rhea Braunstein

Manufactured in the United States of America
Published simultaneously in Canada

August 1994

10   9   8   7   6   5   4   3   2   1
BVG

Contents

Part III   When Caring Is Most Challenging

This is for you, Judith, my wife and best friend.
You died but your love, spirit,
and influence remain with me.
You are my ever-present inspiration.
I cherish your memory.
I miss you, however much you are still here.

Acknowledgments

With this acknowledgment of my friend Victoria Casella, who "pushed" me to write this work and without whose magnificent help it could not have been completed, and the valued assistance of Rick Schultz and my editor Emily Reichert, I close and then open another chapter of my life.

January 1994

Introduction

In a nationwide Gallup poll, nearly half the respondents complained that either they do not have time for their friends or they want closer relationships with the friends they have. Indeed, friendship has become the most neglected relationship of our busy and anxious times. "Friendship" is a rather ordinary word, but it carries extraordinary significance in our lives. We hear about it so often that it is easy to take friendship for granted. Many people do, to their everlasting regret.

Perhaps we need to redefine the term "ordinary" in our culture. To be rich, gorgeous, successful—or whatever—dims beside the stronger lights of being a good friend and having good friends.

I recall a few remarks made by Erma Bombeck in a commencement speech years ago that speak to the spirit of this book. "Most of you are going to be ordinary," she told her audience. "You are not going to the moon. You'll be lucky to find the keys to your car in the back parking lot. But some of you are going to be great things to yourselves. You are going to be the best friend someone ever had. . . ."

Think about that! To be a great thing to *ourselves:* "The best friend someone ever had." It's a secret that has been hidden under the weight of more fleeting and insubstantial values in our culture, such as "success" and "celebrity." But what a truly glorious life goal! True friends make us feel fortunate to be alive, especially during our blackest periods. Indeed, without them we might be lost.

Like most things that are worthwhile in life, real friendship isn't given to us unchallenged and free of obstacles. This book will show that a person needs knowledge as well as empathy to help a friend through difficult times. Some people do the right things instinctively, but at one time or another even they will be faced with challenges requiring specific information about an illness, the process of grief, addiction, and other difficult situations.

Though a chapter or two of this book may not apply to you now, readers can be certain of one thing: At some point in your lifetime, you will confront several of the crises discussed. So hang on to this book. There may come a time when you will need it. There are areas of human behavior that everyone should know about, regardless of their personal experience (or lack of it) with drugs, alcohol, disabling conditions, illness, etc. This book will be of great help in alerting you to a given problem so you can act effectively for your friend's well-being. By increasing our awareness of how some personal difficulties can be endured with style and grace, we take the power away from fear and uncertainty. Instead of feeling awful all the time, we realize we can live through our problems *and* be a good friend to another person who's experiencing a troubling situation.

Though the scope of this exploration has been limited by focusing on how to help a *friend* in trouble, I hope readers keep in mind that all our friends were once strangers. During a recent crisis, for instance, a person I did not know turned out to be a lifesaving friend, one who knew how to help me keep pain, depression, and discouragement from becoming overwhelming. She has become one of my best friends.

One of the messages I hope this book conveys is that being helpful means being well-informed. In many crisis situations, the great enemy is a feeling of helplessness that, unchecked, can easily turn into hopelessness. Friends can combat such feelings through knowledge, which in turn allows for effective and caring assistance.

All of us do the best we can with the information and understanding we have at any given time. I have included specific information and, hopefully, enough resource material to help you help a friend. At the very least you will become aware of alternatives, allowing you to aid your friend in exploring and discovering them for him or herself. "The challenge," as noted family therapist Virginia Satir once said, "is how to give feedback so it comes as a gift rather than criticism."

I have tried to avoid slogans, gimmicky phrases, bromides, and worn-out words of wisdom concerning friendship in crisis situations. They simply do not help. When a friend is desperately looking for a ray of light during a dark time, it's important to remember that saying the *wrong* thing can be insulting or harmful. For example, when was the last time you were helped during a crisis by hearing the phrase "Time heals"? Getting through a difficult crisis should be so easy!

In thinking about this subject, I have discovered that helping a friend in trouble and learning how to accept help from your friends during your own period of crisis or pain require patience, effort, and a willingness to take risks. My hope is that this intimate book—a guide that is also a meditation on the meaning of friendship—will be a worthwhile contribution to achieving those goals. And who knows? When the time comes, *you* may turn out to be the best friend someone ever had.

I hope that I haven't given the impression that it is relatively simple to figure out an appropriate response to a friend in need or a friend in trouble. We certainly have to be careful not to give the impression that we know for sure what a friend wants or needs. There may also be times when we have to distance ourselves from a friend's problems in order to take care of other priorities in our lives. It is not difficult to imagine how painful a situation like this could be. And sometimes you are going to have to face the fact that no matter what you do, it will not change the outcome.

In situations like these it is important to remember that you have not failed as a person (failure is an event, not a person), but sometimes the results are inevitable. It helps to recognize that you can't always be a superhero in someone else's life. It is part of our need to feel balanced in our lives. Finally, we need to be aware—and putting this book together has made me acutely aware—that pain is part of the human condition. There is no way we can avoid pain in our lives, or in those of our friends. The only effective way of dealing with pain is to live through it. Denial, pretending, minimizing, trivializing, and especially comparing problems do not improve the situation. Successfully living through sad or difficult times allows us to understand ourselves and others on a deeper level, paving the way for deeper and more enriching friendships.

This book does not explore the sociological issues. Instead, it takes the personal view, by translating some warm, personal experiences surrounding friendship and difficult life situations into something each reader can use to reshape their *me* into the larger *we*. It is for those who want more meaning than their present life is offering, yet are not sure how to go about making the commitment to be present for others.

I believe a book like this is needed because it has been so very long since we have focused on others. The light of what we knew intrinsically about friendship has grown dim in the face of our "self-development" over the past thirty years. Self-help books will always be popular and needed, but we must now begin reevaluating involvements beyond those that are self-serving. In today's climate, individuals and nuclear families often feel lonely, isolated, and overburdened with their lives. Who can blame them? Whom can they go to for support? Are they even aware that they have the power to help and be helped by others? Reaching out is the kind of risk that has an invaluable return in life satisfaction.

Imbuing our lives with meaning by developing ongoing, lasting friendships is the theme and goal of this book. It is a primer/workbook for friendship, using anecdotal evidence as much as hands-on advice to convey the meaning and responsibilities of these relationships. Friendship is hard work, but worth every bit of energy we put into it.

This book promotes mitzvahs, based on the biblical injunction to do good deeds without anticipation of a "return." It encourages you to pay attention and do the right thing even at the risk of spoiling a friendship. It's a guide to not minding your own business when a friend is in trouble.

PART I

What Friendship Is All About

CHAPTER 1

❦

The Art of Friendship

Forsake not an old friend; for a new one is not comparable to him: A new friend is as new wine; when it is old, thou shalt drink it with pleasure.

—ECCLESIASTES

Yes'm, old friends is always best, 'less you can catch a new one that's fit to make an old one out of.

—SARAH ORNE JEWETT,
The Country of the Pointed Firs

Just a few years ago, millions of Americans identified with the hit film *Stand by Me*, responding to it with deep emotion. The story, based on Stephen King's autobiographical novella, *The Body*, is narrated by an adult (Richard Dreyfuss) recalling his first important experience with supportive friends, as a young teenager. The Dreyfuss character, Gordie, is nostalgic for the risk-taking emotional honesty, loyalty, and intensity of those friendships, which are apparently now lost. The sad part of the story was the implication that this kind of relationship was largely—if not entirely—absent from his present life as a married adult with his own children. The adult Gordie doesn't seem to have any old friends with whom to share the memories of his youth.

For Gordie, friendships once seemed as if they would last forever. Now they're just an excuse for a trip down memory lane. For me, however, one lost friendship is one too many. Old friendships keep us young. If their spirit never dies, neither should the friendship itself. The longer we keep our friends, the more history we accumulate and share together. The more friends see and accept our vulnerable side, our imperfections, the richer and dearer the friendships become.

When I was much younger I was amazed to see older people involved in deep conversation. What could they possibly have to say to each other after so many years? Surely, I thought, by the time people were past fifty or so, they had said everything that could be said. To my delight I have learned that these friendships become more deeply satisfying, alive, and interesting than they had been years earlier. Now that I am living it, I rejoice in this aspect of aging! Since many of life's experiences have already been shared, longtime friends can "cut to the chase" in conversations. New and helpful insights can add depth and color to current situations and important events of the past. Sad times can be shared deeply by friends because empathy has become a natural condition of the relationship. Friends know us well enough to respond to troubled times by helping us find answers within ourselves. When we have a problem they do not feel they have to come up with useless and tired words of wisdom to comfort us. They don't have to be calculating in their responses. Life leaves its mark on these relationships. Understanding and reassurance are offered and also acknowledged in gestures as well as words.

Forgiveness and patience are two of the most crucial components of any lasting friendship. "One of the blessings of old friends is that you can afford to be stupid with them," noted Ralph Waldo Emerson in a journal entry from 1836. Yet that doesn't mean friendship should ever be taken for granted. An Irish proverb says, "Don't put your friend in your pocket," and one from Nigeria says it even more clearly: "Hold a true friend with both your hands."

Tolerance and a sense of humor are the hallmarks of good friendships. The young teens who form the circle of friends in *Stand by Me* have those qualities, and that's why Gordie is so nostalgic in his remembrance of them. Still, the film begs some significant questions: What happens to friendships? Why don't all of them last forever? Why do so many of them drift or suddenly fall apart?

Although there are various answers to those questions, each one reflecting specific life circumstances, the reasons for the breakup or drift of a friendship often center on the most severe test of any meaningful and lasting relationship: how we deal with our own emotions, knowledge, and limitations in trying to help a friend effectively during a crisis, tragedy, or personal trouble.

As the great success of *Stand by Me* indicated and as my own experiences as a psychologist continue to reveal, many people traveling into the uncharted territory of adulthood have begun thinking more and more about earlier friendships. "I wonder what happened to so-and-so?" is a refrain I often hear from them. But I also hear things such as:

"If only I had understood what my friend was going
    through, I could have helped and we'd still be
    friends."

"If I had been less concerned with my own minor and
    more trivial problems at the time, I could have
    helped my suffering friend instead."

The first quote reflects a barrier to friendship: lack of
knowledge and understanding of what a friend was actually
enduring. As you will see in subsequent chapters, knowledge is a central component of caring. Even when friends
try to hide their feelings, there are many things we can still
know about their suffering. Such knowledge generates understanding and, most of all, patience.

The second quote reflects a different concern: the challenge of managing our own problems so we can see when a
friend is in more trouble than we are. A colleague told me
that an old friend who had begun to drift away from him
had called him recently and suddenly said, "I was angry at
you. When I was having trouble a few years ago, you were
selfish and insensitive to my problems. But I don't want our
friendship to drift into oblivion. So I thought about it and
realized that you were probably having it rough too. I'm
not angry anymore. I realize now I expected too much from
you at the time."

My colleague was momentarily thrown for a loop at such
an outpouring of long-held emotional baggage. He recalled
the time his friend was referring to and realized he had
been wrapped up in himself. "I should have been a better
friend to him," he told me. He had discounted his friend's
more serious troubles because he had not yet developed the
kind of sensitivity to others that he now had. He wasn't

ready to be someone's really good friend. But that one call made all the difference: Honesty about his own feelings opened the gate that had been secretly closed between them. It was an obstacle that had kept the friendship from growing and might have ended it. The two men are now great pals, more communicative and attentive to each other than ever before.

It's sadly ironic that some friendships fade. Because of modern technology we can stay in frequent contact with the people we care about, more easily than ever before. Yet many of us admit we don't talk to or see our friends as often as we would like.

Marriage as a Barrier to Friendship

We lose a lot in life by limiting our affiliations to spouses or business associates. The philosopher Bertrand Russell was astonished by married people who condemned the rest of the world "to cold oblivion." An entire dimension of ourselves is neglected when we don't broaden the scope of our relationships. People with friends are invariably more lively and at ease with themselves. They share a range of interests with others. Most committed relationships, whether they are within a marriage, family, or career, become stronger when those involved continually bring fresh ideas and new information into them.

None of us can be all things to all people, even to those we care most about. We can only be the best we can be, encouraging significant others to do the same. That's true caring.

"Friendship is a strong and habitual inclination in two

persons," Eustace Budgell once wrote in the *Spectator*, "to promote the good and happiness of one another." A good friendship is like a good marriage. There is tolerance, nurturing, honesty, and humor.

The opposite of this kind of caring is often selfishness, fear, jealousy, or other controlling behaviors that betray trust or arise from other potentially destructive emotions. Aggressive and abusive behaviors are signs of despair, distress, loneliness, neurosis, and feelings of inferiority. Such behaviors are the opposite of love even when they masquerade as love.

Have you ever noticed that best friends are frequently kinder, more understanding, and more accepting of each other than many spouses are? Best friends don't lie, cheat, hit, or otherwise break the trust that supports their relationship. "Friendship, in America at least, has fallen on hard times," the novelist Reynolds Price recently wrote. "Married adults seldom have close friends or give visible signs of wanting them (though their absence has surely deprived us of an emotional variety that, of old, cushioned the harsher edges of marital contact)."

Spouses often have a romanticized ideal of marriage by which they judge their own relationship. The fact is, when most marriages do not live up to this ideal, little or nothing is done to fill in the void with friends. Unfortunately, the partners mistakenly see friendships outside the marriage as threatening rather than beneficial to them as a couple. That's sad. Many more marriages would survive and grow if the partners would take their vows seriously without also insisting on the fantasy that the marriage be "made in heaven."

Enduring marriages are built on acceptance, honesty,

trust, and love, but not necessarily on spouses having the same interests or friendships. Indeed, there's a lot that's very right in marriages that are flexible enough to accommodate an understanding of people as complex beings with the potential for an assortment of lively, energy-creating interests.

People who explore diverse personal interests tend to live more energetic and fuller lives, and friends are often the spark that ignites curiosity about such self-strengthening pursuits. A spouse may have no interest in learning a new language or how to ski, play tennis, or dance. Yet in a good relationship a partner is usually secure enough about the marriage to not let a selfish preoccupation with doing everything together block a spouse's special interests.

Doing everything together does not usually create a marriage-sustaining intimacy. Instead, it often allows mold to grow on a marriage, developing an energy-draining sameness that slowly but surely eats away at many relationships.

The Terrible Twos: The Couples Syndrome

When a primary relationship ends, either through death or divorce, friendship can become a lifesaver. There's a problem, however, when someone has been inflexibly perceived as part of a couple and when almost every activity took place within the confines of marriage. Divorced persons, widows, and widowers will quickly tell you that they lost many of their mutual friends after they were no longer part of a couple. This is a dangerously lonely position to be in.

Although it's true that most social conventions are comforting in their familiarity and predictability, they can also be deadening. Defying the claustrophobic convention that demands everything be done in couples can let a lot of fresh air into a relationship. Many people's lives would be richer and more interesting if they reflected diverse personal interests rather than merely social status within a marriage or as a couple.

Indeed, pairs can be a problem, especially where old friendships are concerned. My wife, for instance, had a best friend I did not like. It didn't help that I disliked the friend's husband even more. Before I knew what had happened, a cycle had started where we were getting together with these people for one dinner after another. I finally confronted my spouse, and we had a healthy, even necessary, argument. She told me never to bottle up feelings like the ones I had, and said she would be just as happy to see her friend alone for lunch at a restaurant. It turned out that my wife and her friend *preferred* the intimacy and closeness of their private luncheons!

The main point is this: It is not only possible to have individual friends in a relationship, but it is desirable. It's rare when a best-friend relationship extends to the partners. In an immature relationship it's more likely that a spouse will not tolerate a best friend. Issues of possessiveness and jealousy—sure signs of insecurity and uncertainty about oneself and the partner—come out when opposition to a friendship is clear.

I know of a wife who forbade her husband to see his oldest and best friend, who was gay. Though the husband was not bisexual, his spouse felt somehow threatened. She has broken up the friendship, but this act has taken a heavy toll on their marriage.

Forming a Friendship

Developing relationships as insurance against loneliness is not the way friendships flourish. Such calculated thinking implies the kind of selfishness that doesn't usually get a person past the acquaintance stage.

Self-interest can often be self-defeating. Giving without expecting quid pro quo makes mature friendship possible. Over time a friendship develops its own rhythms and harmony. As with other satisfying relationships, we tend to think that the other person gives us much more than we give to them.

Initially we become attracted to people with whom we share common interests, concerns, or beliefs. The primary requirement for friendship is taking an emotional risk by allowing our reserve to drop away. We must be able to reveal our deeper feelings—at our own speed. They are the parts of ourselves that are sacred and unique.

Being open to the possibility of friendship, choosing the right time to allow ourselves to be vulnerable, committing time to the other, and expressing our desire (in words and actions) for the other person to be the best they can be are the primary ingredients of good friendships.

Even when we have a good friendship, there is occasionally a tendency to take it for granted. Maybe we let things get too casual when we forget a birthday, anniversary, or other occasions important to a friend. This kind of thoughtlessness can bring the validity of a relationship into doubt.

Friends will forgive a lot, but there's no getting beyond the fact that they will recall with warmth those times you demonstrated your thoughtfulness by *not* forgetting special occasions. I have a friend who never overlooks such occasions, and she has also created a few new events to commemorate shared experiences. That kind of creative caring, expressed in notes and cards, really does have a powerful effect, especially with friends trying to close the gap of geographical distance. Try it yourself and see if it doesn't make you feel closer and more connected.

Friends don't keep score, but everyone feels at one time or another that a certain friend has given more to us than we have given in return. When I acknowledged this feeling recently, my friend replied that I had given more to our relationship in many small ways over the years. Those acts, whatever they have been, were forgotten long ago by me, but she remembered. It's a curious thing how this process happens! It's like a collaboration in which two partners build something over time. They forget who laid what brick, and when. What emerges is a wonderful, solid, and pleasing edifice: an enduring friendship.

The Art of Worldly Wisdom, written in the seventeenth century by Spanish Jesuit scholar Baltasar Gracián and recently translated by Christopher Maurer, has many wonderful maxims that would be helpful to anyone trying to live well in this world. Gracián has some especially wise and practical words about friends:

> *Know how to use your friends*. It takes skill and discretion. Some are useful when near and others when far away, and the one who isn't good for conversation may be good for correspondence. Distance purifies certain defects that are unbearable at close range. You shouldn't seek only pleasure in your friends, but also utility. A friend is all things, and friendship has the

three qualities of anything good: unity, goodness, and truth. Few people make good friends, and they are fewer still when we don't know how to select them. Knowing how to keep a friend is more important than gaining a new one. Look for friends who can last, and when they're new, be satisfied that one day they will be old. The best ones of all are those well salted, with whom we have shared bushels of experience. Life without friends is a wasteland. Friendship multiplies good and shares evils. It is a unique remedy for bad luck and sweet relief to the soul.

I've always been able to tell when I was in a good relationship. When you have a good friendship your desire to please the other person is just as great as that person's desire to please you, and sometimes more. The friendship is not a trap: It frees you; it enhances your ability to have other caring relationships. The experience is energizing.

Friendships Between Women and Men

Terry McMillan, the author of *Waiting to Exhale*, once wrote about the difficulty of a woman forging a friendship with a man. She persevered, however, and found a real give-and-take relationship in college where she "didn't have to play games." She could be herself: "We appreciated each other . . . without sleeping together."

McMillan points out how rare that is in our society: "Part of it is our parents' fault. We weren't brought up to think of men as friends, only as potential boyfriends or husbands. This is sexist. Why does there always have to be a quest or conquest? We often categorize, even size men up, when we first meet them. Once we eliminate them as potential-anythings, we are open to opportunities which let us establish meaningful, platonic friendships."

Let's extend McMillan's point to two married couples who have been going out to dinners, movies, and plays together. What happens when only two of the four really enjoy each other's company, but the two are the man and woman *not* married to each other? I have seen instances where real friendship can develop between opposite sexes from two different marriages without a threatening sexual involvement. They must be very secure within themselves, however, for this to be acceptable. Their marital relationships must also be trusting and confident.

When Friendships Go Awry

Sometimes attempts at friendship don't work out. Through misunderstandings or misdeeds, we may suddenly realize our friendship cannot develop further. Maybe there are hurt feelings, and anger as well. Feeling bad about friendships that do not take or that quickly break down is certainly normal. It is not healthy, however, to project this negative image of friendship onto your other attempts to develop relationships.

A lover suddenly and callously dropped, for example, may feel that all men are heels or all women are undependable. Yet isolated incidents of betrayal do not mean that they must or will happen again. (If they do recur, does it perhaps mean there is something about you that needs changing?) Seeing people as individuals is the only way we can learn what a person is like. It just doesn't pay to generalize about "them"—regardless of the group!

Assumptions Can Mean Trouble

We make the initial choice of calling a person "my friend." Then we take personal responsibility for our choice by investing ourselves in the other person. We also begin to understand that this person will "be there for us" if necessary. There's a good feeling in the air. Assumptions are made about our friend's ability to help handle our problems and hard times, though we may not be fully aware of something within his or her personality that will make coming through for us difficult.

In one case, a father was having a discipline problem with his child and tried to discuss it with a friend. The friend frustrated him by determinedly taking the side of the child. Perhaps it was a basic philosophical conflict. Maybe the two friends were not able to articulate their positions clearly enough to understand each other. They knew that unless they came to an understanding of each other's position, this "small" problem could escalate and even end the friendship.

More communication was needed concerning the friend's position on disciplining children. Yet if the friend's passion on the subject was taken as a personal affront ("So you're saying I'm the villain? I'm not a good parent?"), bad feelings might come into play, blocking interaction. The friend seemed too argumentative, a quality most people dislike. As it turned out, the friend was—perhaps understandably—not secure enough to reveal a dark secret from his own childhood: He had been brought up in an abusive family where discipline was so badly handled that it left many tortured, unexpressed feelings in its wake. Not surprisingly, what was supposed to be a relatively easy, straightforward conversation about a child suddenly became a serious threat to the friendship.

In this example, time may offer the needed perspective to go back to the friend and say, "You seem very passionate about that problem I discussed with you about my son. I felt you were holding something back from me that could be helpful to our friendship and to my own family situation. You don't have to tell me anything if you don't want to, but if you do want to talk, I'm here to listen now, tomorrow, or next year." Then go on to something else, like a movie you plan to see, or whatever. You have put the subject on the table, and that's the important thing.

However, be prepared for the possibility that discussions about children may not, in the end, be an appropriate part of your friendship—now or ever.

Friendship: No Hard-and-Fast Rules; It All Depends on How It's Done

Sometimes our curiosity about what became of an old friend, or our realization of what went wrong in the friendship, opens the door to a reconciliation and reunion. It's not surprising to hear of renewed contacts with particular friends—either by way of a chance meeting, letter, or phone call—imbuing people with joy, because the great thing about friendship is that it never really dies.

There's a freedom in friendship that few other things in

life offer us. It's a largely unstructured relationship, not depending on social norms and demands that tell us how to be a friend. We can create the occasion for friendship and can be creative in finding ways to nurture it. There are no hard-and-fast rules about it; it all depends on how it's done.

Friends can do a lot for us when they know when and how *not* to mind their own business. They put us in touch with ourselves. Maybe they risked our initial resentment by advising us against a financial transaction we made anyway, or maybe we married and divorced someone our friend was honest enough to warn us about at the start. But when the wreckage of our crisis has finally settled, that friend will probably still be there for us.

Celebrating Friendship

In a way, this book is an affirmation and celebration of long-lasting friendships that transform the ordinary events in our lives by elevating them to a plane of higher regard; they make us feel special. What would the experiences of marriage, a new job, winning a prize, buying a home, or having a baby be like without friends to share them with? The answer: empty.

To have a full, long-standing friendship means eventually dealing with periods where we are investing a lot of time and emotional effort while reaping few rewards. If we have a true friendship, however, such sensitivity and caring are reciprocal. There is the promise that if we stand by our friend, she or he will stand by us.

One theme of this book is that we must expect to give

more than we receive, however much it may turn around in time.

In any case, to establish a close friendship someone has to take a risk. The alternative to this kind of closeness is weaker, more superficial relationships—acquaintances, actually—often reduced to a cost-benefit equation in which returns on investments are calculated.

That's not the kind of "friendship" we will be dealing with in this book, which takes a square, full-in-the-face look at some of life's inevitable and more difficult stumbling blocks to maintaining lasting and rewarding friendships.

There's no doubt in my mind that the person who has one caring, confiding, and intimate friend is richer than another who may have an entire network of acquaintances.

Remembering Judith

Before concluding this chapter I would like to recount briefly a story about my late wife, Judith. Judith was Liz's best friend. Liz detailed to me the critical ways in which Judith personified for her the essence of a "true" friendship. When Liz's husband was fired from his job as a senior executive, Liz was in a state of shock. The experience traumatized her.

Liz and her problems might easily have been written off, since there was no immediate need for her to worry about the economic consequences of her husband's lost position. People who have money, it seems, are often unfairly perceived as unworthy of or in no actual need of help. You can be in real pain, however, no matter what your circumstances. Though Liz had many friends, Judith was the only one who saw the need to comfort her. What did Judith do that was so special? She was there for Liz, she listened and did not judge. Seems like little, but don't be fooled. Friendship, as you will see demonstrated throughout this book, is powerful medicine. Judith's personal attention to Liz gave proper value to the crisis and the people involved in it. It was an act of caring that Liz never forgot.

Another time, when Liz and her husband were tied down by the home care of Liz's ninety-year-old mother, my wife made a point of inviting all three of them to our house for dinner once a week. In addition, Judith made time to find qualified people to look after Liz's mother when she knew Liz and Henry needed to get away and renew their energy. Judith did this consistently until Liz's mother died several years later.

Liz cites Judith's care and devotion in critical times as one of the highlights of her life. Both she and Henry have been enormously helpful and supportive since Judith's death, and they remain my friends to this day.

CHAPTER 2

❧❀❧

Taking Responsibility
in Friendships

Taking responsibility for our friendships means that we care enough about certain people in our lives to put ourselves at risk to do the right thing (as we perceive it) for those people. At times this may mean simply making a suggestion that we believe will improve a friend's life in some small way. In other circumstances we may make a commitment that requires a great deal of time and energy. In all cases the motive is the well-being of our friends, offered freely and without condition. Taking the responsibility to support and assist a friend implies our ability to accept their help should conditions be reversed. In many ways our lives become *inter*dependent (not *co*dependent) and part of a support system that we develop out of our caring and our need for care. These relationships give us a sense of community and the knowledge that we are part of a larger whole from which we can draw and give strength.

In recent years, we as a society have become so sensitive to minding our own business that many of us may have begun to lose our understanding of living in "community" —the good and the bad of it! Everyone used to know everyone else's business. Our behavior was often modified by the attitude "What will the neighbors think?" There were restrictions on what was considered appropriate activity. Many very funny stories come out of that mind-set. Remember when children, on their way to or from school, would behave themselves because they knew any transgressions would immediately be reported to their parents by somebody who was looking out a window or gardening in their yard? If a child did misbehave, there would be "hell to pay" before the first "Hi, Mom, I'm home" could be uttered. The good intention of the neighbor/friend was trusted. How different this kind of "neighborhood watch" is from the one we think of today where people are *asked* to watch their streets as a way to prevent crime and keep neighborhood children safe. Today the idea of minding our own business is taken so seriously that we have all but forgotten the need to watch out for trouble—other than when it may touch us individually. This may be different from how we are with friends, but the essence of the situation is the same. When neighborhoods contained folks who were good friends as well as neighbors, there was an expectation that everyone would care about what happened to everyone else. That "old-fashioned" kind of caring is much less obvious today, although pieces of it remain under a more sophisticated cover. Now we have greater tolerance for individual decisions about child rearing and political and religious affiliations, though (unfortunately) less so for racial, ethnic, and sexual differences. Rather than blurting out what we think about the decisions of others, now we tend to try "problem-solving sessions" with them. When a person we care about is having serious difficulties, rather than offer our "best advice" we try to make personal statements such as these:

- "I'm going to stay in touch just so you know I care."
- "It is important for me to know you are all right. I'm always available if there comes a time when you want me to help or you want to talk."
- "I'm trying very hard to respect your wishes to be left alone, even though it is very painful for me to do that."

While using "I" statements such as these helps to reduce the pressure on someone who is resisting help, sometimes to be truly effective in our relationships, more is required. I suggest that more risk-taking is in order. Be responsible and true to what you are really thinking rather than tiptoeing around. If your relationship is good you will neither make nor break it by gently speaking your mind. If your friend is very clear that your input is not desired, you can always fall back to safer statements like those above. Leave the door open for a change of thinking. Respect your friend's decision (along the lines of this newer thinking about friends), but be sure that she or he is also aware that you will remain a faithful friend.

Often the *timing* of a situation is the most crucial element. There is an old Zen expression that says, "When the mind is ready, a teacher appears." To say it a little differently, "When the mind is ready, a friend appears." If you have already displayed your caring by keeping your focus on the relationship instead of the issue, you have proved that you care for this *person* more than you care about proving a point or being in the middle of someone else's business. This is the essence of friendship.

Sometimes, to make this readiness easier, we need to provide a safe setting. This might take the form of a walk in the woods or relaxing in a cozy spot at home with music in the background. Sometimes it's just sitting together in silence, possibly holding hands. The "safe place" concept is much more important than people think, because it exemplifies sensitivity and a willingness to *provide* whatever is necessary for the other to deal with the problem that needs attention.

Turning a Cold Shoulder

A friend of mine who was very active in his community was faced with a devastating domestic crisis because of the criminal behavior of his mentally ill son. The story was splashed across the front page of a local paper. Just when he needed his friends and associates the most, they began avoiding him. They would not even approach him during services at his church, where he was a deacon. No one even said, "I'm sorry," or "I know this must be a very hard time for you." Perhaps someone might have told him, "I read the newspaper today, and the article about your son was devastating. I can't even imagine how I would feel if this were happening to me." Without ever commenting on the subject of the son's offense, a person's considerate words would have comforted the father. In situations such as this it is not necessary to embarrass anyone or offer advice. Simply acknowledging the hurt would have been sufficient for this man. Another person wishing to do more could offer to spend some time with him and give him the opportunity and a "safe place" where he could just talk about his son and the sadness he was feeling.

Here was a community in which many members clearly needed heart-to-heart resuscitation. They quickly and unjustly wrote off a friend, too easily accepting guilt by association as their excuse for being insensitive. This pillar of the community was abruptly dismissed. Not surprisingly, he stopped speaking with most of his so-called friends. How easily this additional hurt could have been avoided. We find these dramas in many people's lives. How often do we hear on television or read in the paper that when people face misfortune in their lives, they find their friends have deserted them? How often do we read about movie stars and musicians who, when misfortune strikes, find themselves isolated and without friends? Our hearts go out to these people, yet it takes more than sympathy when we are faced with a similar situation and must come up with a personal response—one that requires us to *do* something.

Fear vs. Friendship

Another striking example of this occurred in my own family. My nephew had AIDS. During his long illness, my sister-in-law (also her son's primary caretaker) reported that a large number of his friends remained faithful throughout his illness. However, once the diagnosis was established, one of the mother's childhood friends avoided her. Months later this friend announced to my sister-in-law that she couldn't handle AIDS—the very thought of it was too terrible for her to contemplate. If she had revealed these feelings earlier, my sister-in-law might have understood, but the friend's prolonged avoidance of her and her son changed their relationship. They both lost a precious friendship. One would have thought that after so many years, no circumstance, regardless of the seriousness, could have driven a wedge between them.

This case underscores the importance of being in touch with *ourselves* when a friend is in trouble. Are we ignorant (or fearful) of how to respond to certain diseases or crises? We might be more responsible to our friends by taking some time to examine how and why we feel uneasy under certain conditions. Even if such an examination doesn't reveal the source of our discomfort, we can still tell our friend about our feelings. Maintaining this kind of communication avoids the bad feelings our silence might create. Asking our friend to understand why we cannot be available during a particular circumstance is infinitely better than saying nothing. Our honesty will be appreciated. Trust is built from honesty. This seems all too obvious, yet few people find it easy to act on this simple tenet.

Cranky Friends Need a Loving Attitude

A well-known actress who endured an abusive marriage for a dozen years told me she lost all her friends during this painful time. She realized that she was so ashamed of her situation, she deliberately turned off her friends. Her self-esteem had so deteriorated that she no longer felt worthy of having friends.

When I asked her what she would have liked her friends to do, she replied, "I wished a couple of them had found enough faith in our longtime friendship not to give up on me so quickly." She wanted someone to stick by her during her long crisis, someone who might have realized, "You are not the person I have known. I know something is wrong."

Further, this troubled person wished friends had continued to stay in touch by calling or looking in on her, whether she asked them to or not. Above all, she wished friends had realized that when she was ready, she would have let them help. This woman's sad story is all too familiar. Still, it brings up a point too seldom understood: True friendship is durable enough to survive even a friend's bad behavior. To have a friend who is still available for reconciliation and forgiveness after an ordeal is a great blessing.

Little Things Do Count

Sometimes people feel that doing a small thing for a friend isn't enough. One friend, for example, was guilty about just being at the funeral of my mother. He had merely made himself present and available to me. It was such a comfort to have him there that I was puzzled when, later, he told me he was sorry he didn't do more. I was surprised, because I felt he had done enough. Now, many years later, I still recall his thoughtfulness, his loyalty, and his friendship.

To all my readers, I say not only please *don't* mind your own business when a friend is in trouble, but also please *do not underestimate* the strength your mere presence carries for someone you care about. It may seem like a small thing, but just being there for a friend speaks volumes about what true caring is all about.

The Constructive Power of Friends

It comes as a shock to many people when they learn how much constructive power they have to affect a friend's life for good. I recall the story of a friend's twenty-three-year-old daughter who, unbeknownst to her family, had used all manner of drugs and then finally became a heroin addict. Though her family had noticed she was losing weight, they never suspected drug abuse was the cause.

Here was a young woman who knew all about the dangers surrounding drugs. During her teen years she had sworn she would *never* get involved in such self-destructive behavior. One morning, after eighteen months of living on her own, she called her mother in tears. The desperation in her voice was alarming. After much questioning she admitted her problem with heroin and revealed that it had been going on for seven or eight months. Her family rallied to her side and, with her consent, enrolled her in a rehabilitation program. So far she is doing very well and has remained drug-free, finding new friends and new employment.

The reason she called home in the first place was the intervention of a friend. She had spent the day prior to her lifesaving call home with someone who didn't mind his own business—he listened to her story and understood her pain. This person convinced her that she needed her family's help to change her life. Fortunately, he turned out to be the only real friend among her companions. The rest of her pals were, like her, too out of touch with reality to understand what was actually happening to them. The daughter now says she will be forever grateful to him, realizing that his patient concern for her was *truly* lifesaving.

It is not always easy to know who will be a friend, to what extent a friendship will grow or be an important part of your life. Every so often people we think will be wonderful companions come into our lives. We hope they will give us something special: a feeling of togetherness, a shared interest or hobby, an ability to laugh. Our desires for friendship are unique, although most of us want the feeling that "we have clicked" with another person.

It is rare to find someone who can fill all our wants for a friendship. However, the closer a person comes to the "ideal" we construct for ourselves, the more likely the friendship will last over time and become a truly life-altering experience.

This is not meant to minimize the importance of friendships with people who will never be our best friends but who may fill important gaps in our relationship spectrum. Most of us regard as friends some people we don't feel "connected" to on a deeper level. Yet we enjoy their company and share common interests. They give our lives variety and enjoyment, and their influence is a positive force.

Over the years I have spent a great deal of time thinking about friendships. Only in retrospect have I been able to develop a list of the qualities that have been most important to my lasting friendships. Those tried-and-true friends share the following characteristics:

- They are willing to nurture my growth.
- They can be trusted.
- They are patient and forgiving of my mistakes and inadequacies.
- They are there and available when I need them.
- They have a capacity for playfulness and humor.

- They are intellectually stimulating.
- I feel good about myself in their presence.

How do you become a good friend? Be someone others can rely on. Be there for them. While we cannot always interpret correctly what friends are feeling or what they need, we do the best we can. As time passes we will know more about our friends and make fewer mistakes with them. At times true friendship might require us to intrude and confront, even at the risk of losing the friendship. This is particularly true when addictive or violent behavior is an issue. It is difficult to be a friend when there is an imbalance in some aspect of their behavior. Often we just don't know what to do. The best response is to become introspective, put ourselves in our friend's shoes, so we can more easily determine what we would like a friend to do. More than likely we will be right on target with our action on their behalf.

The impact we have on friends is often unknown to us. We will feel great joy if at some time someone tells us, "If it weren't for your caring friendship I would not have been able to . . ." Conversely, we may get hit with the negative side of that coin should a friend blurt out some long-forgotten slight or omission on our part. You can almost count on this happening even in the best of friendships. Before resorting to defensiveness or anger, try to appreciate the underlying feeling. Since we already know we would not deliberately hurt or harm a friend, the worst we will have to do is apologize and claim our lack of sensitivity. No one would want a friend to conceal bad feelings about them, so this kind of clearing the air can have a positive effect on the relationship. Certainly it can lead to a greater understanding of the other person, which, after all, is one of the goals of friendship.

In friendship there is a mirror of responsibility. Everything we want from others, everything we expect them to be for us, is what we must try to be for them. Our intention is the growth and welfare of others, and this is reflected back to us by them.

CHAPTER 3

❧

Barriers to Good Friendships

Most of us can recall a situation when someone we thought was our good (or even best) friend deserted us for another, stole a boyfriend or girlfriend, or blamed us for something he or she did. The feelings we have from events such as these last many years. We have been betrayed, and our faith in the goodness of people is shaken on a very personal level. Henceforth our decisions about trusting others are more difficult and tentative.

I would like to appeal to people who have had disappointing experiences to reevaluate their situations and not punish themselves for circumstances that were not their fault. This might also be a time to ask the forgiveness of a friend you may have hurt.

Sometimes attempts at friendship fail. Through misunderstandings or misdeeds we realize our friendship cannot develop. We have hurt feelings and anger toward the person and/or the circumstance that caused us to lose something precious. Feeling bad about this is certainly normal. It is not healthy, however, to project this negative image of friendship on others. Isolated incidents do not mean that all or even most people will be disappointing as close friends. We can never generalize about people; we are each unique, notwithstanding some shared traits.

Getting but Not Giving

If others let us down more than a few times over several years, we may want to look into the way we choose friends. I remember a former student who always chose her pals for the wrong reasons. Not surprisingly, she did not recognize or understand that fact. Instead, she blamed everyone but herself for her lost friendships. She often felt angry and betrayed. Carrying around so much negative emotional baggage made her less attractive to potential friends. Still, she desperately wanted these relationships.

After many unhappy and lonely times, she had an "ah-ha" experience about herself. She realized she was always trying to develop friends who would do something for her. She *expected* friends to do more for her than she was willing to do for them. Who wouldn't tire of that rather quickly? No one she ever met! In any case, she started looking at people differently, noticing qualities in them that she liked and respected. She put considerable energy into not allowing herself to develop an agenda for a new friend's behavior. She decided *her* loyalty to a friend was at least as valuable as that person's loyalty to her. In effect, she started looking at others for who they were and less at herself and her needs. She found many new ways to *be* a friend. The side benefits of this new attitude were considerable: She liked people more, and she was happier.

Turning Regret into Friendship

When the wife of a close friend died in a tragic accident, Don didn't know what to do. Now, many years later, he feels guilty about not responding in some way to his friend's grief. Don is my old friend. I know him to be a sensitive individual, so I had to ask myself a few questions: What happens to friends when they are faced with a crisis that demands from them a little extra strength and caring? Why is it so hard for many people to find that emotional, social, and psychological footing necessary to help a friend in trouble?

One of the typical responses people have to a crisis is understandable. You have heard it; maybe you can recall saying it yourself: "I just didn't know what to say." If I had a nickel for every time I heard that regret while composing this book . . . But Don revealed another dimension to that unhelpful response, and he was able to tell me about it. "I was very upset myself," he said, "but thought my grief would appear trivial compared to my friend's. In a strange way, I also thought that my saying anything would result in his breaking down and weeping and I wouldn't know how to respond to that either."

Don was talking about feelings of helplessness and about his own discomfort with strongly expressed emotions. A crisis often makes us feel helpless because it signals a lack of control. A drunken stranger runs into your friend's car; there's an earthquake in which many people die. No wonder we have trouble even *thinking* about such events! But they happen, and in thinking about them we can regain some measure of personal control over our response.

When events occur outside our control, there's no need

to let feelings of powerlessness dominate us. We can turn around such feelings by finding out what we can do to help, and then doing it.

There's no getting around it: Digging into some unpleasant life experiences helps us discover why truly caring friendships are so vital. In helping a friend overcome adversity, we find the places where human dignity, honor, and enduring love reside.

A Crisis Is Not Forever, but a Friendship Can Be

It's important to remember that no matter how bad your friend's crisis may seem, he or she won't be living in it forever. There will be time to understand and help a friend in trouble, even if you did not get it right from the beginning. A friend's trouble may hit us with the suddenness of an earthquake. It's understandable if we are thrown off balance, but be assured that there will be time to gather forces and help. Don't let a crisis scare you off!

Adjusting to a friend's crisis does not happen all at once. It occurs naturally over time. Be confident that new routines can be established around the changes and conditions generated by the crisis. These changed conditions, however, do not mean that your friend has changed. He or she will be essentially the same person you have always loved —with the same qualities that initially brought you together. Maybe your friend's sense of humor will be the first thing you notice that's still operating quite well. If so, go with that part, but at the same time be aware of and attentive to the feelings underneath the humor.

For example, a young friend who lost his first child joked with me only two days after he endured a long ordeal in the hospital. His daughter's lung had not formed correctly; she died after four agonizing hours. "Oh, if only it had been flat feet!" he told me with an ironic smile, acknowledging nature's capricious ways.

At first the humor put me off balance, but then I realized that my friend's sense of humor—his essential personality—wouldn't change overnight. I knew that his humor, in this instance, covered the fact that he was hurting badly, but I went with him. I acknowledged his witty philosophical point with a smile. Humor was one way he was trying to organize and understand his thoughts about what had just happened to him and his wife.

It is interesting to note that if I had been put off by my friend's seemingly odd attitude about his loss, I might have taken it as a cue to drift away from him. Patience was important, and so was timing. I realized he wasn't ready yet for an intimate talk, but he didn't want to cut off communication with friends totally. So he kept a safe distance by joking. A month later, he was ready to talk. All the pain poured out, freeing him from so much he had been holding inside.

Incidentally, today he is the proud father of two healthy children, a boy and a girl. He still has his wonderful sense of humor, and we're still good friends.

Getting Back in Touch

Relationships with many disagreements can be as frustrating as they are satisfying. The lively discussions are almost always attempts to have someone we care about understand us. Differing views on issues such as politics, religion, or money change as we grow and become "wise." Growing and changing along with someone who understands our heart (as well as our thinking processes) can be among our most treasured experiences.

One person I interviewed for this book told an unusually poignant story about how he handled a crisis in a friendship. He and his buddy had a good relationship from the time they were in elementary school. In their twenties, they found they were disagreeing, frequently and on many subjects. Their political and social views were very disparate, and their way of talking about these subjects was usually loud. They decided they liked each other more than their differences would indicate. Nonetheless, their constant "discussions" were beginning to wear on their relationship. Since they met at least once a week, they agreed to talk only about their philosophical conflicts rather than current events. After six months of *really* listening to each other's point of view (including many hours taken just to determine what they *meant* when they used certain words), they felt closer and had a firm grasp of how the other thought. Their respect for each other increased; they understood the *reasons* for the positions they held. They found their beliefs were actually quite similar, but they chose to express their social consciousness in dissimilar ways—and they used language differently.

This man said it was the worst and best six months of his life. It was the worst because so much pain was involved in their talks. (He also said that the discussions caused him to reevaluate critically everything he believed about his life.) It was the best time because he and his friend reached a breakthrough point after about four and a half months. Then they put all the pieces back together and found themselves strong—and caring. They are now in their fifties, and their friendship is stronger than ever. Their respective spouses agree that this friendship is life-enhancing for everyone involved, not just the principal characters.

Fear of Being Asked to Do Too Much

There are times in life when rough situations come back-to-back. We think we will not be able to cope if anything else disrupts our lives. Imagine that you have just been through an unusually difficult period, but as fate would have it you are now being asked to focus on a *friend's* crisis. Certainly we are all entitled to healing time. Even though our reluctance to give ourselves over to our friend's need would be understood, we must still try to do the best we can.

In his classic book *On Caring*, Milton Mayeroff points out that caring is not "simply a matter of good intentions or warm regard":

> . . . in order to care I must understand the other's needs and I must be able to respond properly to them, and clearly good intentions do not guarantee this. To care for someone, I must *know* many things. I must know, for example, who the other is, what his powers and limitations are, what his needs are, and what is conducive to his growth; I must know how to respond to his needs, and *what my own powers and limitations are.* [Italics mine.]

We all have known people who are afraid of caring. Chances are they fear giving because they aren't sure they're strong enough to set limits. "There's no end to giving," they may have said at one time or another. Caring entails risk. Though it makes us human and gives our lives dimension and fullness, caring also makes us vulnerable. Yet friendship, especially in a time of crisis, shows us that when we distance ourselves from pain—for whatever reason—we distance ourselves from love. There is no substitute for having friends. Even in the best situations, where a loving family is present, very little else enhances life more than a good friend.

The bottom line is this: We all need good friends. The problem is that we can't just *have* a friend, we also must *be* one to have one, and that takes some effort. Putting a higher priority on friends, allowing more time for people you care about, is a win-win proposition.

A Friend in Need Is a Friend Indeed

Perhaps the not-so-hidden agenda of this book is to suggest that none of us can afford to lose even a single relationship through neglect—regardless of how uncomfortable we might be about responding to difficult circumstances that affect the lives of those we care about. But respond we must, for our own sakes as well as for those with whom we associate. We never know when our own lives will take a problematic turn and the support of friends will be a saving grace. The good news about responding to friends, even though we are not sure of doing the right thing, is that 98 percent of the time we do exactly the right thing as long as we focus on their needs.

The Balance between Self-Sufficiency and Need

Some people build a wall of self-sufficiency around themselves at some time or other in their lives. They say, "I'll be fine," or "Don't trouble yourself, I can handle it." Though they never seem to need anything, they're always ready to lend a helping hand when you are in trouble. When these people do require assistance, however, it is more likely that their needs will be harder to see and therefore easier to ignore. The efficient Hannah in the film *Hannah and Her Sisters* gave and gave, but in not allowing others to give back, her relationships stopped being mutually rewarding. This is a good example of a block, or barrier, in a friendship.

Friendship is easier when it is mutual. Part of the healthiness of an alliance is finding the balance between the two poles of self-sufficiency and neediness. A self-sufficient friend can at times make us feel as though we are not really needed or of value during stressful times. Try to be honest and strike the balance. Reveal your feelings and ask your supercompetent friend to work out a compromise with you —give you a chore that will allow him or her some time to relax and you to feel useful. No matter how skewed the roles each of us play in the relationship, they are rarely a reason to give up a friendship. Invariably areas of mutuality exist, along with the loving feelings, to make such a friendship worthwhile.

On the other hand, an overly needy friend can be a drag. We're not talking about a friend who may be dealing with a terminal illness, but the one who constantly emphasizes their problems or any litany of negative events. Although a true friend often endures such trials, relentless pessimism severely limits rapport. Recognizing the situation might motivate a caring person to challenge the other gently to an hour of "good news only." If it works, the time could be extended the next time you meet. Who knows? Given enough time, your friend may develop a better way of relating.

Many people have trouble admitting they could use help, because they think it's an admission of helplessness. Others may find it threatening to ask for help in a crisis, preferring to suffer. The possibility of rejection may prevent them from asking for assistance. Yet it takes a *strong* person to make such an admission. Even Cheri Register, a writer suffering from a chronic liver disease, once said she had a note taped to her refrigerator that read, "Feel free to ask for assistance. Friends are willing to help if they know your needs." But do you know what her comment on this was? She said, "Yet I hate like crazy to do it."

Why Do People with All the Answers Make Me Feel Awful?

When I ask you to listen to me and you start giving me advice, you have not done what I asked.

When I ask you to listen to me and you begin to tell me why I shouldn't feel that way, you are trampling on my feelings.

When I ask you to listen to me and you feel you have to
do something to solve my problems, you have failed
me, strange as that may seem.
Listen! All I asked was that you listen, not talk or do—
just hear me.*

One of the most serious barriers to helping a friend in
trouble might be called the know-it-all factor. Know-it-alls
seem to have all the answers to our problems. If it involves
a crisis in our family, they tell us we should do this, or that.
In the case of our grief over the loss of a loved one, they
may offer clichés such as: "Time heals," "Get on with your
life," or "You should think of dating again." Easy to say—
too easy to be of any help to a friend in trouble. Such
know-it-alls need to learn to listen, feel the sentiments of
the other, and keep a tight rein on all advice and judgments.

Since a crisis or tragedy in a friend's life affects us as
well, we may feel the need to define and possibly *control*
the subsequent confusion and hurt. Instead, be a sensitive
listener. A friend's emotional, physical, and psychological
pain has little in common with our sympathetic responses
to such pain. We may think we know how it feels to deal
with his or her problem, but we really cannot know. We
may have clues, but that's all. Assuming more is risky business.

Though we may quickly reference another friend's crisis
with a story of our own, it's best to remember that such a
strategy helps *us* more than our friend. There's an unavoidable advantage to such responses, because we are bringing

* Author unknown.

up the memory of a situation from which we have had some time to heal. Though this is understandable, it can set up a barrier between friends. Remember, your friend's pain is fresh; his or her sadness, unique.

It is important to realize that at some point all of us will be a friend in trouble. Such times need not be completely black periods for us. When someone close stays with us through tough times, helping us the best way he or she can, something unforgettable occurs. Being a true friend and having one may seem ordinary to some people, but these times of endurance and overcoming obstacles are usually among the high points in anyone's life.

Helping to Remove the Barriers Others Are Facing: When a Friend Is Stuck

Friends can be uniquely helpful in situations when someone is having a difficult time getting some important task or life work started or finished. Most of us have experienced this problem. It may seem like a case of procrastination, like the dental appointment that is put off—indefinitely. Or the breast exam that never takes place. But I'm not talking about simple procrastination here, I'm talking about *stuck:* the novel or article that sits in your friend's drawer because of writer's block, the dissertation or thesis that has not been finished. Perhaps your friend can't quite begin the training needed to compete in a marathon, find a new job, get help to overcome a relationship rut, or take an overdue vacation.

Whatever "it" is, here we are dealing only with situations that your friend *wants* to do something about, that are to his or her advantage, and that do not hurt or exploit anybody. Here, too, we are *not* operating on the assumption that the failure to do what is needed is based on what people call "deep-seated psychological problems."

"Stuck" means life interference. "Stuck" means a slow, often harmful assault on your friend's self-esteem that reflects on his or her ability to feel competent and in relative control of life. In many cases, such as an incomplete college dissertation, "stuck" can have a lifelong impact on your friend's career. Without a completed dissertation, there is no degree. Without a degree, a friend's career ambitions could be paralyzed, immobilized, finished.

What can you do for your friend? The best approach (and I've been there before) is to be present for your friend. Offer to help him or her get started with whatever is blocking forward progress. Sometimes getting unstuck may mean getting started on an insignificant aspect of the task. Or it may be accomplished by simply changing the environment. Here are a few things you might say to help jump-start your pal's stalled objectives:

- "I'll go with you to find a new apartment."
- "I'll go to the library with you and help collect the research."
- "I'll train for the race with you."
- "I'll go with you to the doctor. Let me make the appointment for you."
- "We'll brainstorm together and, you'll see, you'll start writing" (or "You dictate to me," or "I'll get it transcribed for you").
- "We'll have a credit-card-cutting party."
- "Why don't you come over for dinner and bring

      your work with you? Later you can work at my
      desk."

- "How about taking a weekend off to relax? Don't
  even think about [the problem], then attack it fresh
  on Monday."

Such suggestions may give your friend just the needed
push to start the process of getting unstuck. Of course, you
will need to be there to help for the follow-through. Make
it your project. Say, "It's painful to me that this hang-up is
having such an effect on your life. It's interfering with our
friendship. We need to get it out of our way. Haven't you
noticed how much time and energy you use in wanting to
do [fill in the blank] but *not* doing it?"

The key, of course, is always your presence. Make it
known that you see what's happening and that you care
enough to help. This is one of those times when you can
strengthen a relationship, when your time and presence
will mean the most. Take advantage of the opportunity.

Here's a page from my own experience. I was working on
my Ph.D. dissertation at the University of London. It was
an extremely painful, boring experience. I just couldn't get
with it. My college roommate (also my best friend), Brian,
was desperate. He was fed up with my preoccupation about
the dissertation and lack of productive work, which greatly
interfered with our plans for leisure activities. We were
both passionate devotees of music, theater, and especially
the ballet. It was the heyday of Margot Fonteyn, and my
roommate was especially annoyed when I didn't "have the
time" to do my share of waiting in line for tickets to her
performances. The more he nagged, the worse I got. Then
he came up with a brilliant idea. He intensified the friend-

ship. We were to go out *every* night either to a play, a concert, or a movie (tickets were *very* cheap in those days). He proposed a "reward-and-punishment" strategy. Whenever I worked for two hours, I got a reward of one hour. We had fun mapping out the schedule, and it worked. Not only did I finish my dissertation, but Brian and I enjoyed seeing almost every play, movie, ballet, and concert London had to offer.

I have since suggested a modified form of this reward-and-punishment strategy—successfully—to several good friends who were stuck. It convinced me that sometimes people just need a little push, not professional treatment.

Many of us have friends who are very stubborn. It may be hard to decide if they are stuck or if they are just being remarkably persistent. One friend of mine, Peter, is a fine painter. The problem is that he has not been able to sell a single painting to anyone but me. That sale wasn't charity. He is truly a talented painter, and I consider his work far superior to the popular paintings that sell very well. To the conventional art world, he doesn't amount to anything. To me, Peter is an artist.

What does someone do, however, when he sees a wonderful friend failing to earn a living and dependent on family or friends? Sometimes the role of a friend is to be practical and help him or her make productive compromises. I encouraged Peter to finish his degree and get a job as a teacher, so he would still have time to paint. Eventually he acted on this suggestion; now he is independent and self-supporting. Recently Peter has experienced a measure of public success by having his paintings accepted for an exhibit in Holland and New York.

CHAPTER 4

❧

Reconciliations and Reunions

In her wonderful novel *Perfect Happiness*, Penelope Lively observes that "Passion spends itself—oh my goodness, does passion spend itself—but friendship is always there. Like a good marriage it survives attack." This is an ideal view of a good friendship, and though it's often true, everyone can relate to the experience of having had one or more truly excellent friends with whom they are no longer close. It's strange how friends enter and exit our lives. Some people I know have said they don't even remember what caused the breakdown of their relationship.

What happens when a friendship drifts away, or when it seemingly ends? In reflecting on this question I had a painful memory of breaking up with one of my dearest friends. My reasons for ending the friendship, I now see, were petty. Yet my reasons seemed important enough at the time. Now, older and wiser, I have a whole new perspective on the subject.

Sometimes, of course, there is actual deception or betrayal among friends, but even so, could we begin to think about forgiveness? I should explain here that I am not big on forgiveness for every evil act. Forgiveness is appropriate when we consider that people are imperfect, make mistakes, are immature. But many times it is appropriate to take revenge—knowing full well that the best revenge is living well. When a friend of mine wrote to me asking for forgiveness for misjudging my motivation about revealing a confidence, I was too enraged to accept it. The timing wasn't right for me, and when I did try to reconcile some years later, it was too late. He had died tragically in an accident. It is interesting to note that during the Yom Kippur (Day of Atonement) services, Jews ask forgiveness from God for the sins they have committed against God. This plea for pardon does not include sins that have been committed against another person—those infractions need to be forgiven directly and personally.

It is difficult to substitute the warm feelings and connection of an old friend—a person you have known for a long time and with whom you have established certain traditions and rituals. Having laughed and cried together and celebrated significant milestones in your lives bring wonderful feelings of "being one with the world." If you have an old friend from whom you have been separated for some silly or serious reason, you might wish to take this opportunity to recall some of the shared times and feelings and make a move toward reconciliation. In doing so, however, be willing to risk the possibility that your friend may not be ready to reciprocate. If the timing is not right, the mind will not be ready. Despite this possibility, he or she will know you want a reconciliation and can respond in kind—when ready. That first call is very difficult, but the door is unlocked thereafter.

I'm personally very fond of Ann Landers, and I especially liked it when she suggested a "Reconciliation Day" in one of her columns. At the time she paraphrased something Toni Morrison said, and it went something like this: It doesn't really matter what was done to us; generally hanging on to the hurt victimizes us, not them. If we want to heal we must take the old manure and fertilize the flowers.

As I get older, I find myself more and more anxious to pay attention to my old friends (in a strange way this made it much easier to make a few new ones), but there is something about the passage of time and especially the testing of friends in a crisis situation that has made me appreciate the power and the joy of friendship more than ever.

Let me tell you about one experience of a reunion that brought great joy into my life. When I was in the army I made a really good friend. He was, in many ways, my salvation. I was unsuited to the military life. I missed the familiar territory I called home and the availability of the theater and the arts. Bob and I met by accident, and I can remember to this day how lucky I felt to have finally met someone who didn't drink and didn't womanize. More than that, he read books and wasn't opposed to the opera. Wow! We got along famously and enjoyed many lively discussions. We lost touch after we were transferred to different duty stations. Although I wrote frequently after my discharge, my letters were returned, and his were never received by me. How do I know? Some forty-eight years later, Bob's wife, Lois, read an article about me in a YMCA publication. Bob had spoken about me (as I had about him to my wife), she showed him the article, and the result was a grand reunion. We exchanged life stories and were delighted to discover that we both became psychologists, and although our other interests were not similar, we both still enjoyed each other's company, even after so many years. What a joy to find a lost friend!

CHAPTER 5

❧❀❧

Friends in Difficult Situations

In the course of life we become involved in many personal relationships. By reading, by watching people we admire, or by hearing the stories of others we come to some sort of understanding about how to behave when a new or unusual circumstance comes into our lives. We learn to apply our past experiences to new situations.

Certainly the way we were brought up influences how we react to the needs of friends. It gives us a base from which we develop our own individual responses to those closest to us. Even if we have serious problems with how we were raised, as adults we try to learn different living skills and a code of ethics that fit our personal belief systems. In our relationships with others we tend to reinforce these beliefs—either by associating with people who think as we do or by learning and incorporating new information from them. Despite this, at times we find ourselves caring about people who engage in unexpected, even surprising behavior or who are faced with dilemmas about which we have little experience. We have to decide how we are going to respond, using a new set of guidelines.

In this chapter I offer several situations in which we can help friends through difficult times. The circumstances beg us to think about how we might respond to those we care about when the circumstances are new to our experience, difficult, possibly embarrassing, or potentially life-threatening. Though the situations may not apply to your life at this time, I think that some of the thoughts and questions the circumstances provoke will point to ways in which you can develop into the type of friend you want to be—and have! Whatever you do in a sensitive situation, there is always a risk that the friendship could be wrecked. I am suggesting that all really meaningful friendships involve your time, caring, attention, empathy, and a willingness to risk the relationship for the sake of what you believe is "doing the right thing."

Risky Business: To Tell or Not to Tell

What do you do if your best friend is about to marry someone you don't like and you know in your heart that the marriage will be a tragic mistake? In our society half of all contemporary marriages end in divorce and about 60 percent of all second marriages fail as well. Given these statistical realities, and what you know of your friend's relationship with her boyfriend, you believe she has no chance at all! You feel you must say something. There needs to be preparation for possible tension, so before you talk to your friend, prepare.

What I'm getting at is that people need to learn about and discuss this business of love and marriage before getting married. Once a friend is "in love," it's very hard to influence that person not to enter into a marriage for the wrong reasons or with the wrong person. More often than not, "madly in love" becomes just plain "mad" after a few months of marriage. This philosophy is elucidated in my book *Why Love Is Not Enough*, which could serve as a basis for discussion.

Let's move ahead. She is about to announce her engagement to this "bad news" fellow. He is sometimes violent, he lies, and he often drinks too much. Sure he is gorgeous, charming (most of the time), and appears to be rich. Could you handle a conversation like this? "Look, Mary, you are my best friend. Can I tell you what I think about Joe without making you angry? I mean, without spoiling *our* relationship? I have to tell you first that I won't mind if—in fact, I hope—I'm wrong. If you go ahead with the engagement, I'll be with you all the way as though we never had this conversation. However, I am worried. . . ." And you tell Mary about your doubts concerning Joe.

Friendship during a difficult time may depend on how well the people learned to understand each other when times were good. Speaking at times in "what ifs" helps them to clarify their feelings about the relationship. For example: "How would you feel if I see something in a boyfriend [girlfriend] of yours that you don't see? Should I say something? Would you become angry, and would it spoil our relationship? Should I keep quiet?" Defining the boundaries of the friendship while there is objectivity will give you both the "nerve" it takes to protest when a personal and subjective situation arises. Even when people understand each other very well, it is still risky business—be sure you and your friend have either agreed that there are no conditions on the friendship *or* that some subjects are taboo.

Once, while I was speaking to a group of about one hundred students, I asked them, if they had bad breath, would they want their friends to tell them about it. They all raised their hands. Then I asked if anyone knew people with bad breath. Again, all hands were raised. Last, I asked if anyone had ever told their friend or friends when they had bad breath. Not one person raised a hand! Interesting?

A young friend of mine recently remarried after a horrendous six-year marriage that was full of dread and despair. He revealed that several of his good friends had known the first wife quite well. From the start of his relationship with her, the friends couldn't imagine it working out. Still, not one said a word to him. Among the reasons were: "I didn't want to hurt your feelings." "I was afraid it would spoil our friendship." "You seemed so much in love!" When I asked him what would have happened if they had spoken to him, he wasn't sure, but he thought he probably would have married her anyway. Then we discussed how he would respond now if a friend of his was about to marry the "wrong" person. He felt he would risk a conversation similar to the one outlined above. It's a lesser risk to the friendship if you have evidence and are well-informed about why so many marriages don't last. As we concluded our conversation, my friend acknowledged the possibility that a friend who had taken the risk and told him the truth would now be trusted above all others.

The Power to Change Situations

Readers may recall the story of the New York City train driver who, while on drugs, was involved in a fatal accident. His coworkers and friends knew he was a drug addict. This is the kind of sad story that occurs thousands of times. Why? Is there any way to prevent such tragedies from occurring? Are there times when friends have such power within their grasp? The answer is a resounding "yes," but it takes the risky, albeit potentially lifesaving, intervention of friends to slow or stop another friend's path to destruction. Easier said than done! Even parents who know of the drug abuse of their friend's son or daughter often do not say a word. There are friends who know when a driver is drunk and do nothing. What about a friend who knows absolutely about the sexual or physical abuse of another but chooses not to report it? We call these people "enablers"—they have allowed themselves to be part of the problem instead of being part of the solution.

When something tragic happens, friends rationalize their inaction with statements such as, "I wouldn't betray a friend," "I promised I wouldn't tell anyone," "He would lose his job," "She'd never speak to me again," or "It was none of my business." It's okay to protect our friends, but are we sure we know what we are protecting them from? Are we letting ourselves be blinded by our definition of friendship to the detriment of ourselves, our friend, and others?

What about issues such as dieting, smoking, or gambling? Anyone who has friends has at least one who is on a diet or smokes too much. Let's use a constant dieter as the prototype of the point I want to make, which could apply to any problematic situation of a person who is concerned about the well-being of their good friend. Current research suggests that about 90 percent of all people who go on diets fail. In many cases the brief success of a diet does more harm than good. In the long run, dieters often end up with more weight than before their diet, not to mention the added sense of failure they feel. It's not difficult to appreciate that people overeat to relieve tension or depression. When friends concentrate on the symptoms, they often make matters worse, and their intervention can jeopardize the relationship.

Powerful Aids for Bad Health Habits

What to do? Intensify the relationship! (This is a theme to remember in many difficult situations.) Believe it or not, friendship is a powerful diet aid. At the point when you decide to help—really help—your friend to reduce, you should be at a high point in your relationship. See your friend more frequently, call more often, write more often (no reference to the weight, smoking, etc.). Extend more invitations, such as "Let's take a walk together" or "How would you like to go for a swim?" Invite him or her (with significant other?) to your house and serve a gourmet meal with *delicious* desserts designed especially with minimal calories (yes, such desserts exist).

As a special treat give your friend my book titled *Life Is Uncertain—Eat Dessert First*, coauthored with Harold Brecher. You read it first. You'll be surprised by its message. If at any point your friend says, "You are trying to trick me into losing weight [not smoking, etc.]," make a point of acknowledging your culpability with remorseless flair! Then say, "We had some good times, didn't we? Besides, as an alternative we might have had a scene, and I hate scenes, *but* I love you!" Then give your friend a hug.

It's not within the scope of this book to get into all the controversy about compulsions vs. addictions or what makes people behave the way they do. I'm pretty sure, regardless of the circumstances or therapeutic interventions, that very little progress is made without the healthy ties of friendship and family.

Sometimes You Win, Sometimes You Lose

Here's an example of a tacky, and pretty risky, situation. What if you have a good friend who has been having an affair (unbeknownst to you) with another friend. The wife of your good friend is now seeking a divorce after twenty years of marriage and three children still at home. The wife is also a very good friend. They *all* say to you, "Either you are supporting me or you're not my friend."

In this situation, my friend was indeed having an affair with another friend, the wife was outraged, and all three insisted that our friendship depended on whom I chose to support. I tried to take a neutral position. The outcome: I lost all three of them as friends. Sometimes your best effort isn't good enough. Sometimes no matter what you do, it will result in the breakup of a relationship. Frankly, sometimes you just can't know what to do.

A Friend Who Has a Mentally Ill Child

Mental illness is something most people find difficult to talk about. Even a friend who has a mentally ill relative avoids the subject because of embarrassment or an unwillingness to bring up a touchy topic. How can you become close to someone if you can't talk about certain subjects?

This possibility may seem remote to you right now unless you already have such a friend, but in any given year, according to the National Alliance for the Mentally Ill, approximately 1.8 million people are diagnosed as schizophrenics, and more than 10 million people suffer grave depressive disorders.

I asked my social worker friend Mona, who has a thirty-five-year-old schizophrenic son, how she would like her friends to relate to her (the son lives in a group home, but there are frequent visits). The first thing Mona said she wanted her friends to understand was that this was an unending travail for her. There is no time when the agony or distress of the situation is not present at some level. She wanted her friends to know that there are times when it's painful to be asked how her son is, but then she realizes that there would be one thing much worse—not to be asked at all. Mona believes that denial and shame are among the most destructive factors in families with a mentally ill member. She is sometimes overwhelmed by and grateful for extra-special kindnesses (such as good friends visiting her son while she is away at a conference or on a lecture tour). She has reached a point in her life where she can have a good time, wonderful friends, and experiences without any formal acknowledgment that her son exists. Her good friends, Mona says, seem to know when to ask about her son, can listen when she talks about him in detail, and accept those times when she responds perfunctorily that he is fine.

Mona says she lives a good life. In her work she is able to help other people who have mentally ill children. She has a caring family who have accepted her son, and she has several very good friends. Is there any message she would like to get across to the general public? Maybe it is a small thing, Mona replies, but mental illness is an illness, and when the person is hospitalized it would be nice for friends and family to visit and bring flowers.

Your Response?

A good friend is faced with a terminal illness and has been told by three different physicians that he has just four months to live. He won't accept the prognosis, and he moves into massive denial, including the refusal of all but minimal treatment.

You know there are many authenticated stories of people beating the odds and surviving years longer than they were supposed to. Denial and hope may facilitate the healing process, but they are rarely cures. Even so, if this adds a few months to *living*—why not? Even if this works with a small percentage of terminally ill people, can you go for it?

Denial does not mean you do nothing. A "we'll lick this one" approach may require a lot more work and energy than settling into an attitude that admits "there is no hope." What often emerges is that a patient with hope—with a sense of humor—will get the needed support of friends (and, indeed, medical personnel) more readily than someone who is depressed, irritable, or downright nasty (however much we might understand these feelings).

My reading of the situation is that many of the startling successes of the "New Age" practitioners are grossly exaggerated. But again, "miracles" do occur. I believe that people who don't believe in miracles are not realists. I'm hedging, of course, because even the Talmud says, "Expect miracles but don't count on them."

I certainly would not support the nonsense that people with AIDS or cancer actually will it upon themselves or that they can just will it away. I also suspect that as many people die "prematurely" from denial as live longer as a result of it. Except in unusual circumstances (such as denial of medical treatment to a child because of religious convictions), it must be the patient's choice.

A strange and perhaps unrelated story comes to mind. Some relatives of mine were awakened in the middle of the night during their vacation by what was obviously an earthquake. They quickly ran out of their room to get outside as the entire hotel was swaying. As they ran through the lobby they saw a young girl on her knees, praying. As my cousin rushed by, she scooped the girl up. My cousin said, "Run now, pray later!" Minutes later the entire hotel collapsed. Fortunately, all those who evacuated the hotel escaped unharmed. If nothing else, the story does suggest that attention to reality still counts!

How Will You Respond?

For the past year, about once a week or so you have been going out with a friend from work. Whether it's a movie, a play, or just sitting in a bar to discuss work and the meaning of life, you have a good time. Today she becomes quite serious. You ask if there is a problem, and she says, "I am a lesbian, but I'm still in the closet. Can I trust you with this secret until I have the courage to tell the rest of the people I care about? You are my 'test case' in terms of coming out. I want to be open, but I need some time and support before I tell my folks and the rest of my family."

This could be a confusing time for someone whose images of gay people come only from television news programs (e.g., demonstrations by activists and gay pride groups, the speeches of religious fundamentalists who call homosexuality a sin, and interviews with psychologists and sociologists who say it is inborn) and from casual conversations with people who understand about as little as you do about this phenomenon. Never have you had to take "acceptance" so seriously or so personally.

- Can you do this for her?
- Will her sexual preference change your relationship? Why or why not?
- Does her homosexuality shake any of your beliefs and, just as seriously, your feelings? How? Why?

How will you respond? Are you going to have to redefine yourself in some ways? The answers are tied into your sense of security, of course. The questions become: What kind of a friend are you? Will you say yes—and be open to learning? What is important here?

Let's look at the issue of homosexuality from another perspective. Suppose your best friends' very dear and only son, who is seventeen, a star athlete, and has been dating, announces to his parents that he is homosexual. The doting father is devastated, and the mother is ready for the hospital. Their first reaction is to pull him out of the private school he has been attending and pack him off to a psychiatrist. As a witness to their distress, you can assist if you help them focus on the relationship to their son. Try something like this: "Listen, you don't want to make matters worse, so you can't reject or alienate your son. Aren't you even slightly pleased that he trusted and loved you enough to tell you? Many kids don't feel they can tell their parents, and that leads to more problems. It is to your credit that he felt he could talk to you. You don't want him to run away, or worse, commit suicide. I really think you could help the situation if you try to remain calm, talk to him about this, and let him know you love him for himself, for the wonderful son he has always been."

Parents and friends need information and support. Suggest they get in touch with Parents and Families of Lesbians and Gays (the address of which is listed in the Resources section of this book, along with information on several helpful publications).

Yet Another Tricky Situation

What if your best friend has been involved in a financial scandal? You know he is guilty. He asks you to post a high, not easily affordable bail, and he has already hinted that he might have to skip town.

If you cannot afford to lend a friend money, it's better to say, "Perhaps I should lend you the money you asked for, but if I did, I wouldn't be able to meet some of my own obligations. I couldn't do that. It just is not feasible for me to neglect my personal needs and responsibilities, even for you."

In this particular case, you need to recognize that the friend you are worried about is his own worst enemy. No one gains by weakening the standing of another. Since there are constraints on what you can do, you can talk to your friend in terms of your own limitations rather than his "best interest." Deal with your values, feelings, and limitations.

On the other hand, there's no getting around the fact that sometimes the offer of money is the best medicine in saving a friend. When a "miserable pinch" was over for one man and his family, he wrote to thank his friends for lending him money:

> This act of kindness did me an unspeakable amount of good; for it came when I most needed to be assured that anybody thought it worth while to keep me from sinking. And it did me even greater good than this, in making me sensible of the necessity of sterner efforts than my former ones, in order to establish a right for myself to live and be comfortable.

The man, Nathaniel Hawthorne, became one of America's greatest authors, but his friends could not have known that in 1849. They took a risk. Maybe they expected to lose the money. Who knows? Hawthorne's situation was and is not uncommon. Perhaps your own friend needs a temporary loan to get through a "miserable pinch."

However you handle the above situations or variations of them that you'll eventually confront, it's important to remember that good friendships develop with shared experiences, with the accumulation of memorable times during which trust and faith in the relationship are built, more than with "favors." Good friendships survive long years when *all* that has been asked has been answered—even when the necessary response did not comply with the need of the other person. Honesty and trust have been the consistent qualities of the relationship.

Caring inspires friends to find ways to enhance the life of the other during good as well as difficult times. There is no one lesson in this chapter, but by now it should be clear that we need to think about how we interact with our friends. It is a great challenge to be a true friend. If you are in your relationships with friends for the long haul, then you—and they—will take every interaction seriously and with concern for the other.

No lifelong friendship will be without trials or times of misunderstanding. The basic principle to keep in mind is that even after the anger, disappointment, or the "I'll never forgive you" statements, there will be a need to repair the friendship. Loss is hurtful. No matter what happens, you always can say, "I want reconciliation and forgiveness because I love you."

PART II

~~🌸~~

When Not to Mind Your Own Business

Sometimes the Right Thing to Do Is to Mind Someone Else's Business

TODD: You want me out?

NEAL: No, I want you in. But being in means you gotta do something, not just say you're in.

TODD: Listen, Neal, I appreciate this concern, but I'm not like you. You say things and people listen and I'm not like that.

NEAL: Don't you think you could be?

TODD: The point is that there's nothing you can do about it. So you can just butt out. I can take care of myself. All right?

NEAL: No.

TODD: Whatd'ya mean, no?

NEAL: No.

—*Dead Poets Society*

CHAPTER 6

❧

Violent and Abusive Situations

When violence is a part of personal relationships, we are shocked. We usually attempt to deny the amount of violence in our country, making it the "odd circumstance" that disrupts what we like to think of as our peace-loving society. But if peace and charity begin at home, then apparently we have not made much progress. Recent publicity about the high incidence of domestic violence (physical, emotional, and verbal) has shocked many, but I suspect others (the victims of abuse) are saying, "It's about time." The violence that is carried out, primarily on women and children, and mostly behind closed doors, has become a very serious public concern that crosses all ethnic and economic boundaries.

To emphasize this, here are some statistics about this type of abuse that were printed in an article highlighting one community's effort to stem the tide of domestic violence:*

* "Too Scared to Go Home," San Francisco *Chronicle* (July 8, 1992).

- A quarter of the women in the United States—more than 12 million—will be abused by a current or former partner sometime in their lives.
- 47 percent of husbands who beat their wives do so three or more times a year.
- Rape is a major form of abuse in 52 percent of violent marriages.
- Based on FBI statistics, 30 percent of women who were murdered in 1990 were murdered by husbands or boyfriends.

High-risk victims are:

- Women who are single, separated, or divorced
- Women aged seventeen to twenty-eight
- Women who abuse alcohol or other drugs or whose partners do
- Women whose partners are excessively jealous or possessive

Battered women are:

- 23 percent of those women who are pregnant and seeking prenatal care
- 25 percent of women who attempt suicide
- 25 percent of women seeking emergency psychiatric care
- 19 to 30 percent of injured women in emergency rooms

If you, the reader, are involved in a violent relationship, please, please understand that it is *never* your fault. There is no excuse for this kind of violent behavior. If someone hits you or rapes you, he does *not* love you! Violence *does not* demonstrate caring. If you believe violence is okay within families, or others have told you that slapping, hitting, punching, and raping are a "man's right" within his home, then you must learn new behaviors. Stop it in your generation—*do not* let your children think such destructive and humiliating acts are acceptable.

Thoughtful Caution Is Necessary When Helping

To be a friend to someone who confides to you that her spouse or father or brother is (or has been) abusing her takes special patience and cautions. Don't do anything that will place you in danger of the abuser's violent behavior. Do *everything* you can to help your friend, but only with her permission. For instance, you should never try to force your friend to move out of her home. You can tell her that you think she would be better off without this constant threat to her safety, but until she believes you, your beliefs may not be in her best interest. Does this mean you should not talk to her about the situation? Not at all. You can always reinforce your willingness to help when she is ready. (Call 1-800-333-SAFE to find the nearest shelter—be prepared for the time when your friend is ready to leave.)

You can do a great deal to help your friend feel competent and confident that she can do well for herself should she decide to leave the destructive relationship. Ask questions about the abuser. Find out if he is violent toward anyone besides her (children, his parents, etc.). If you know the person, watch for verbal abuse and put-downs that undermine self-esteem. If you witness this behavior, be sure to tell your friend, in private, that she does not deserve to be treated that way. Do nothing in public that may make the home situation worse for her. She needs long-term support much more than your interference during a single incident.

Do not challenge an abuser's bad public behavior unless you are reasonably sure you, or anyone else who intercedes, can stay in control. Be careful to approach the person in a calm manner, without personal insults. As an onlooker, you don't know why or how this person became violent, nor can you shame a person into change. Counseling is the best setting to help people overcome inappropriate, violent behavior. Abusers need this kind of help more than anything.

You can also familiarize yourself with the locations, capacity, policies for confidentiality, etc., of shelters for abused women and children. (In some places the location of shelters is kept secret from the general public. If this is the case, you need to talk to the agency or agencies that sponsor shelters so you know how to get in touch with the people staffing them.) How do the local police treat domestic violence cases? Do they have access to counselors and support systems for abused children and adults? Ask those you talk to about other resources for obtaining help. More and more communities have agencies that focus on assisting people who either have abused or feel they might abuse their loved ones. Parenting classes can help a great deal when the adults in the family only "know" about raising children from their own abusive households.

Above all, maintain the confidence your friend has in

you. She may want to ensure that no one else is aware of the situation. Respect her decision. You never know at what time she will decide to change, and you will certainly want her to trust you to be her friend when that time comes. Read *When Love Goes Wrong . . . What to Do When You Can't Do Anything Right* by Ann Jones and Susan Schechter (HarperCollins Publishers, Inc., 1989). It contains just about all the information someone in this situation needs.

When abuse involves the child of a friend, your involvement is much more compelling. Here again, as I have often emphasized, strengthening the friendship is the key to pushing your friend into getting help. Protecting the child may become your first priority and you may be forced to intervene with protective services even at the risk of jeopardizing your friendship.

If you have a child whose playmate seems unusually bruised or has many "accidents," watch the child carefully and try to determine if there are some behaviors that would indicate an abusive parent. Call a crisis line, get information about the resources available, and try to get the name of a child advocate. Laws and policies in certain cities require investigation and follow-up regardless of whether the information about abuse is fact or hearsay. Before you act on anything to disrupt a family's life, be aware of the consequences—to them and to you. Not many social service agencies are equipped to deal well with abusive situations. Some make matters worse. Therefore, except for blatant and obvious abuse, it's best to explore other routes—tell a local clergyman, ask questions (anonymously, if necessary) of child-abuse experts. They must know that your concern is sufficient to require assistance. Don't do anything that will expose the child to even more harm.

If Your Friend Is Raped

> . . . my outlook was bright in those days. Everyone around us appeared content, happy, hopeful. Friendships were coming together. . . . Close by, within a mile of us, a man I had never seen before was about to turn forty. I cannot imagine him surrounded by hope and friends and smiles as I was. I cannot even imagine him smiling. Life must have seemed very dark to him. Unimaginable pressures must have been building: rage, hopelessness, distorted reality, pain. Soon, he would force all of these onto me.*

Late one night your friend calls, crying hysterically, and you have trouble understanding her words. Finally, "He raped me!" becomes chillingly clear.

Go to her immediately. If she objects because it's very late or "too inconvenient," ignore the protests. If you live so far away that going to her is impractical, ask if you can call the rape crisis line in her community. After you explain the situation to them, have someone from the rape crisis line call her.

In either case, tell her *not* to shower, change clothes, or do anything to her body until she talks to the people from rape crisis or to the police.

* Migael Scherer, *Still Loved by the Sun: A Rape Survivor's Journal.* New York: Simon & Schuster, 1992.

Assuming you are near, allow her to talk until she has calmed down enough for you to say, "I will be there in _____ minutes." If she doesn't want to hang up the phone, ask her to call another trusted friend or the rape crisis line and talk to them until you get to her. When you arrive, allow her to experience her own feelings. Sometimes the person will appear emotionless because of the shock of this violation. Don't encourage emotions or try to suppress them; accept without challenge whatever the person is feeling. (I don't know if this happens to you, but when someone tells me to "go ahead and cry" or "let it all out," I can't.) When she seems ready, suggest a call to the sexual-assault unit of the police department or the rape crisis line.

Even if this was a date rape and your friend is unsure about pressing legal charges, she needs to be examined. Her decision to press charges can wait, but evidence of the attack needs to be recorded officially. This is an extremely difficult process for a traumatized woman. She may decide not to press charges against the rapist. But if this same person rapes again, she may well change her mind. The report from that initial examination will become crucial evidence. More important, the physical exam will begin the medical process used to determine the presence of any sexually transmitted disease or pregnancy.

The best outcome to this offense is that the person who was raped has understanding and supportive people around who will listen and empathize with her. If recovery seems unlikely even after a prolonged period of time, urge her to get professional help or to join a support group.

A good friend will not "allow" a rape victim to blame herself for the rape. Sometimes a person will find herself in a situation where she is vulnerable to attack—after several drinks, in an isolated place, etc.—but that does not excuse the attacker (be it stranger, date, or spouse). Be very clear with your friend: Rape is not something a woman "asks for"! Being in an unsafe circumstance never implies permission to be violated. Nothing can transform this act of violence into one of consenting sex or "making love."

If your friend was physically injured there are some very practical things you can do. Help with the nursing care, bring meals, take her to support groups, accompany her to the doctor (after hospital care), and, as always, allow your friend to talk about the experience. Help her think of activities and plan outings that will help her to begin to look to the future.

The emotional consequences of a rape can be horrendous. As Migael Scherer observed in *Still Loved by the Sun*, a deeply sensitive account of her own rape and its aftermath, even her own sister did not understand what she needed. "Her words, so well intentioned, hurt deeply," Scherer writes about a letter received from her sister. The sister had told her to "Drop the obsession with the man who raped you. . . . It isn't right or healthy. Get the best professional help you can. We all want you back."

Sounds heartfelt, doesn't it? Scherer wasn't fooled, however. She heard more loudly "the words between the words" in her sister's letter, an impatience that said rape was "something to 'get over' as soon as possible, rather than to assimilate slowly and naturally." Scherer knew that her sister was just "impatient with my pace. And . . . tired of hearing about *it*." The author wishes family members had been able to stay with her during her slow process of healing. She would have hoped for a response of "gentleness and vulnerability," rather than unfeeling, analytical impatience. "Evil is real," Scherer concludes. "Good is just as real." Good friends are stronger than evil. They stayed by her, providing her with the crucial additional strength to keep going forward.

Spousal rape is finally being recognized as a crime. If your friend is raped by her husband she has some very different and difficult decisions to make. In this instance, it is a time for her to consider what to do about her life, over and above recovering from this abusive event (especially if it's not the first time). Support her the best way you can. Be available to talk and "brainstorm." Listen to her sorrow about her life and her hopes for a better future. Encourage her to get counseling for herself and her husband, regardless of whether or not they stay together. People who hurt their loved ones need serious help.

Friends along with counseling and/or therapy groups play a major role in the recovery process, which may extend over a long time. If your friend does not seem to be healing at all, the level of professional help or peer support may need to be increased or changed.

Even with a close support group of husband and friends, for example, Scherer reports great relief after calling a Seattle rape center and speaking to a counselor. Feeling there should be a time limitation to her healing (six months? ten months? more than a year?), the author was told there are no timetables or shortcuts. Like Scherer, your friend will be glad to hear from an experienced counselor that eventually she will be close to herself again. A counselor can also offer sound advice, like this given to Scherer: "Practice being yourself again, if you're up for it. Do something for your own pleasure. Spend a little time with people who know nothing of what happened, just for the escape."

Friends can do a lot to help recovery along, but no one can hurry it. It takes time for a rape survivor to believe that the intense psychological pain will eventually fade. Even so, the memory of the rape, and feelings surrounding it, may last a lifetime.

Even distant friends can have a profound effect during a terrible crisis. Indeed, one sensitive letter can provide strong and significant support for a suffering friend. Migael Scherer prints a beautiful letter she received from a friend who was living in Alaska. The letter arrived about two months after a rapist almost strangled Scherer to death. It gave her hope and strength during a particularly rough time. Here is how the letter to Scherer closed:

> I hope, Migael, I haven't presumed too much in saying anything. Our culture doesn't seem to have a standard way to express respect for another's suffering, except by silence. (In Asia, you can bow to the person.) I didn't want to keep silent about this; you should know your friends are with you.
>
> David

It's a fact that men are also raped, and not only in prisons. Males who are raped report the crime even less often than females, because of their overwhelming shame. While it's true that women are victims of rape more frequently, male rape can be just as complex and terrifying, requiring precisely the same level of sensitivity as shown to women.

People who have been traumatized within dysfunctional families or by other past experiences will be much harder for friends to reach. They often require therapy. There is no evidence, however, that psychoanalysis or other long-term treatments are more effective than short-term counseling. My own recommendation is to help an abused friend seek out a cognitive-oriented or rational-emotive therapist. Rather than targeting the traumas of the past, both treatments focus on responding in a rational manner to events in a person's present life.

Friendship during such sadness takes on the air of the holy. It takes a great deal of commitment to be a true friend during such desperately trying times. There may be no reward, but when love is offered, hope for positive change is possible.

Here are some important points to keep in mind:

- Rape is rape; no one "asks for it."
- A physical exam is needed for health and legal reasons.
- Professional help may be needed for recovery.
- Recovery may take a long time. There is no set timetable.
- Violent husbands who rape or abuse their wives need help to learn healthy ways to interact with women. Most grew up with abusive people.
- Friends of rape victims are very important to their recovery.

CHAPTER 7

❦

Good Friends Who Have Problem Children

What can you do for parents who have a child who is giving them a lot, and I mean a *lot*, of trouble? Let me address the issue from the perspective of the parents—your friends. It may give you the insight you need to be helpful.

First, do not always accept the proposition that a difficult or "bad" child is a consequence of bad parenting. It's often not true. No one can say with any degree of certainty how the home environment, genetics, and society affect a child. It's important to have a sense of just how deep the issue of problem children goes before you can approach the situation with a helpful attitude. The parents will probably need your understanding most upon the realization that their problem *child*—now perhaps a young adult—is *not* going through a phase, a stage, or an age of change.

Maybe your friend has tried counseling for his child, bailed him or her out of trouble, covered up bad behaviors, offered total love, given support and forgiveness. But what if, after all the worrying, shouting, pleading, agonizing, screaming, crying, and even praying, the child has become worse? What if he or she is now into drugs, alcohol, or promiscuous sex?

Here's a representative portrait of what your friend may be dealing with. Some of the pieces of this terrible picture may fit your friend's situation. This person may be enduring a child who is defiant, angry, intimidating, depressed, passive, dysfunctional, or mentally ill. The child may be flunking out of school or college, unable to hold any job. Lying, threatening, and stealing may have become all too frequent occurrences. Sleeping and eating patterns are *way off* center. The child is clearly out of control, dominated by any number of I-can't-help-it compulsions, yet she or he seldom fails to blame one of the parents for this behavior and despair. Many out-of-control children are masters of manipulation.

What does such a portrait of the problem child mean for your friends? Well, chances are, they are emotional wrecks. No doubt the situation has them feeling guilty, inadequate, depressed, and angry. Life is nightmarish; it's like being stuck on an emotional roller coaster with little hope of ever getting off. I have known several cases over the years where professional friends—whose job it was to be helpful to other people's children—had very difficult children of their own and felt completely inadequate in their parenting roles. They felt like phonies. Life, for them, became especially unbearable.

At some point your friend may experience one of the most painful events in life: rejection of their child. Actually, most of the time it's the *other way around*. The child has abandoned or rejected the parents. Most mothers and fathers do not reject or abuse their children. Mistakes have been made, of course, but basically most parents try to do the best they can. They love their child, but eventually they must confront those inevitable and shamefully held feelings of hate as well.

Parental love can be defined mainly in terms of when a parent's desire to meet the child's needs is more important than meeting his or her own. *When a parent's effectiveness in life begins to falter through emotional exhaustion or crippling frustration, so does any hope of acting out of love.* Your friend will eventually have to accept the fact that a child's destiny can't be totally controlled, nor can parents be completely responsible for the child's mental health, emotional well-being, and sociability. It's not easy. Parents take pride in the achievements of their children. Some even measure their own success by the success of their children. When their children are doing well, no one asks why. It's just taken for granted. When children are in deep trouble, however, all the fingers point to the parents. But it's the self-accusations that are most damaging, and they are even more devastating when the parents blame each other.

Often it is not possible or even important to pinpoint cause or blame. Some fancy therapists claim they know the answers to problem children, but the best available research suggests that the fancier the theory, the more speculative the explanation. In my forty-plus years as a psychologist, I've seen healthy, well-adjusted families with severely maladjusted children. I've also seen adults living fuller and more healthy lives than the abusive, rejecting parents who "raised" them. The way—and to what degree—parents influence a child's life remains a mystery.

We simply don't know why some kids are more influenced by peer groups, the media, and drug experimentation than others. Why, in one family, are there two wonderfully adequate, respectful children and one who is a horror show? Theories and explanations aside, who knows the truth?

Helping to Let Go of the Problem Child

A time may come when helping means encouraging the parent or parents to learn how to let go. It's a process, and it's not easy. Few parents can be expected to let go of their problem child all at once; it's an emotional seesaw that takes time. Make no mistake, letting go is *not* giving up—it's not done out of hate or retaliation. It starts by accepting most of the statements presented below. Essentially, these ideas are used as pledges. The parents will need them to create positive change within their lives. As a friend of someone with a problem child, you need to know them as well so you can reinforce and support your friend's efforts. Here is a parent's pledge list:

1. I'm fed up. I'm ready for change. It's not going to be easy.
2. My way has not worked.
3. I can tell that even if I knew the cause, it wouldn't help much, if at all.
4. I can't control or change my child. I can change only myself.
5. I'm finished blaming—attributing blame is just not helpful to anyone.
6. I'm not going to deny the pain. I just can't let it control my whole life.
7. I'm finished nagging, screaming, crying, and plea

bargaining. I'll concentrate on my own problems and responsibilities.

8. I'm not going to pay attention to research studies or articles that blame parents.

9. I will remember that difficult children don't choose to hurt their parents. They can't control themselves.

10. I will try very hard to understand that my suffering does not alleviate my child's problem. My life will be real and mine again. I will "fake it until I can make it."

11. My situation can be an incentive to be more sensitive to the personal tragedies of others. I must always avoid being sanctimonious.

Suppose your friend still cannot make any constructive moves. That's understandable. It's all so much easier said than done. Help your friend find out about available counseling, parents' groups, and books that might help get the process started. Talk it over.

If your friend is not ready for these direct approaches, try an indirect route by encouraging him or her to:

1. Learn something new—take a class, develop a new hobby.

2. Be helpful to someone more vulnerable than himself or herself.

3. Volunteer two hours a week with an organization *un*related to "the problem."

4. Improve the relationship with other members of his or her family.

Encourage your friend to try a month of giving "the problem" some distance. Instead of attacking or pleading, suggest your friend try "I" messages once in a while. This means saying very calmly and without anger, "I was scared all last night because you didn't come home or call," or "I'm upset because you were drunk again. Go clean up your vomit, I won't." "I" messages can be especially effective when they're kept to one or two sentences. "I'm terribly frustrated because twenty-five dollars is missing from my wallet." "I really appreciate seeing you sober. Let's go get some ice cream." These messages help us recognize our own feelings and keep us focused on the moment. We get into such trouble when we dredge up the past all the time! (There is a time and a place for this, but usually it doesn't help the present circumstance.)

Unfortunately (though understandably), all too many parents fall into patterns that are the opposite of "I" messages. Especially unhelpful is "You're no good," or "You'll never amount to anything." Just as destructive is "How could you do this to me?" or "You'll be the end of me." Such comments are to be avoided entirely.

At some point your friend will be ready to get his or her life in order. This doesn't mean that all or even any of the problems will be solved. It means getting ready to deal with them in a less stressful and damaging way. The whole idea is to assist friends in making peace before *they* go to pieces.

If your friend decides that an experimental period away from the chaos of his or her problem child is a good idea, you might suggest that the following paperback books be taken on the journey:

The Different Drum by M. Scott Peck

When Living Hurts by Sol Gordon

When All You've Ever Wanted Isn't Enough by Harold S. Kushner

Man's Search for Meaning (revised and updated edition) by Victor E. Frankl

How to Stubbornly Refuse to Make Yourself Miserable About Anything—Yes, Anything by Albert Ellis

Both you and your friend could read them carefully and critically—for an hour or so a day—while going about your other tasks. Although the journey I'm talking about might be an inner one, a real vacation or even a few days away during this "experimental" period would make it even better. It's not important to agree with or share most of these authors' ideas. Just go for what is inspiring. Some ideas will cling.

One of my favorite books is *The Way of Man* by Martin Buber, a brilliant analysis (through the medium of Hasidic tales) of love and spirituality. However, no book will change your life—only you can do that. The artist Corita had a poster that said, "Love is hard work." It is! My imaginary poster announces, "Change is hard work." It is!

Things Your Friend Can Do to Relieve the Tension

First I'd say, "Make peace, beginning with yourself." Forgive yourself. It doesn't matter how many mistakes you've made, how much you feel responsible for your child's behavior. Hate, bitterness, jealousy, and irrational guilt only tear at your guts. They're exhausting. You need your energy for today and tomorrow. If you can't forgive yourself now, *pretend* you can. Meaningful change takes time, so pretend for now. What harm can come?

You could suggest these ideas to your friend:

- Write a pledge to yourself—a poem or song.
- Remind yourself of the pledge by keeping a log or a diary.
- The repetition of certain thoughts can become potent medicine:
  > "I shall either find a way or make one."
  > "I will be gentle with myself."
- Perhaps "The Serenity Prayer" will do it for you:
  > "God grant me the serenity to accept the things I cannot change, the courage to change the things I can, and the wisdom to know the difference."

Here are a few ideas to stimulate insight or discussion. At some time you will be ready to focus outward and work on forgiving at least one person who has hurt you. It may be a parent, spouse, another child, or your (former?) friend. Forgiveness frees your energy. Though love may return, it may not. For now, focus on letting go—being open to forgiveness. Usually the bravest step after forgiveness is being polite. If there are one or two people you *can't* forgive, get revenge (the best revenge is living well). Especially if your own parent or parents abused you, living well means *not* doing to *your* child what was done to you.

As more time passes, you will be prepared to take a new approach with your problem child, no matter how remote that seems now. Gather your own support group. If your marriage is strained, *un*strain it in little ways. Start with "Maybe it's my fault." You don't have to believe this 100 percent—just be open to the possibility. (Go along with all the minor suggestions your spouse makes, such as "Let's eat out tonight" or "How about a movie?" You may not want to do those things, but you're after a "climate" change, and saying "Yes" helps.) It seems contrived because it is—it needs to be—until "nice" things come naturally and with spontaneity. Intensify your relationships with friends, other family members, and anyone else you can think of, until you have the support system you need. This may take a while and be difficult, but it's better than the "self-destruct" attitude previously used. Avoid making critical decisions while upset. If provoked, you can say, "Honey, you are making some valid points, but I need time to think about them. Please be patient with me." Safeguard your health. Exercise. Eat for nutritional value. Be moderate in your activities. Rest.

When you feel like you have your balance back, have a serious, nonthreatening talk with your child, or write a letter something like the one below:

> Dear _____,
>
> What has happened to you may be partially my fault, or maybe it's nobody's fault. I just don't know anymore. In the process of fighting, we have hurt each other. We have hurt others as well. I hope you'll forgive me for whatever responsibility you feel I have regarding the direction your life has taken until now. What can we do to make things better between us? Stop talking about the problem? Agree not to talk

when we are angry? What are you willing to do to change the situation? I want to make compromises so we can get along better. We will always be here for you, but that does not mean you can ignore our needs. Your behavior affects all of us. We see you hurting yourself, and your outbursts, stealing, etc., are hurting everyone.

I have finally realized that only *you* can help *yourself*. Only you can change yourself. If you want help, I'll help you get it. I will always love you, no matter what you do, but that does not mean we can continue living as we have been. Let's get together (you name the time and place) and talk about this situation as calmly and respectfully as possible. There must be some small changes we can each make to start the process of healing our wounds. I really want to try and hope you do too.

> All my love, always.
> [Signed] _____

Use the above letter to ignite your own thoughts and emotions as they apply to your unique situation. If the first "meeting" works out okay, try for a family conference. In any case, by making sure your destructive child knows you have set limits and mean to enforce them, you have now moved out of the problem and into the solution. No matter what response you get—and you may not get any—you have made a healthy and effective start at getting *your* life back on track. The best result would be that you each make one or two promises to change particular behaviors that "irk" the other.

By the way, a sensitive book for parents who still can

influence their children in conventional ways is *Between Parents and Teenagers* by Haim G. Ginott.

Where Teenagers Are Concerned

Though some teens come to think of adolescence as the best time of their lives, for others it's an especially heavy trip. Your friend will worry about the maturing child, but maybe you can help him or her turn the worry into a productive concern. Children live in a society where the majority of adolescents experiment with drugs and/or sex at one time or another. These are the facts. Such early risk-taking and attempts to be outrageous usually do not have any serious consequences for later adult development. Surveys have shown that the majority of teenagers do not perceive parents, teachers, or counselors as good sources for comfort or the solution to problems. Many youngsters report that the best relief for unbearable upsets, tensions, and even minor disappointments is listening to rock music or, more seriously, having a drink or smoking a joint.

While most teenagers manage to negotiate their way through such confusing times, there are clues or signals that may be sent out by those who are *not* coping well. Try to be sensitive to them. There's a big difference, for example, between outrageousness as *theater*, as an exaggeration that makes many adolescents feel special or noticed, and outrageousness that flirts with violence and danger.

If a behavior reaches a compulsive point of "I can't manage without it," as in substance abuse or cruel behavior, then quick action must be taken. Children or young adults who inflict gratuitous cruelty on animals should always be a source of serious and immediate concern to parents and their friends.

Should a child or young adult show some of the following behaviors, substance abuse may be the problem. Here's how a psychologist and mother characterized her own child:

- He doesn't talk about feelings.
- I can tell there is all this pent-up rage—but he's always denying it.
- He lies a lot.
- He chooses friends badly.
- He's very conformist in dress.
- He can't tolerate waiting or frustrations and wants immediate satisfaction.
- He can be very charming, engaging, and cute.

This mother was able to conclude that her son was becoming an alcoholic. Time proved her to be correct.

Young People and Alcohol: A Few Key Messages

I'm offering some key messages we need to get across to young people. I wish schools would convey these messages, instead of offering useless courses and dumb slogans such as "Just Say No!" to their students. Most important: A friend should learn to recognize the effects and dangers of substance abuse.

My key messages for young people are:

- If you drink or get high, don't drive.
- If someone says in a loud, abrasive voice, "I'm not drunk, I can drive!" he or she is drunk and shouldn't drive.
- If one or both parents are alcoholic, consider this a possible early warning sign. It's best to avoid drinking altogether.
- Alcohol, drugs, and smoking are like poison to the unborn and can lead to a variety of birth defects that drastically affect the health and mental abilities of a baby and the mother's life as well.
- One small mistake, such as driving while drunk, can affect your entire life: It can kill you, and it always puts the lives of others in danger.
- One or two drinks can, as Shakespeare wrote, "Provoke the desire," but more than that will "take away the performance." Impotence (the inability to maintain an erection) often occurs in sex after drinking too much.
- Chronic alcoholism can begin after just one year of heavy drinking. You begin to act like your own worst enemy, and you seriously damage your brain, liver, and stomach. An early death (twenty-six or twenty-seven is not unusual) can be the result.

CHAPTER 8

❧❀❧

Addicted Friends: Intervention

There is something I've discovered about alcoholics and other addicts to sex, drugs, and gambling. As a one-time therapist, most of the addicts I've known—and they number in the hundreds—have appeared to be nice, lively, interesting, and often very talented people. When addicts begin to deteriorate, however, a different "character" emerges. The most important fact a friend must appreciate about virtually all addicts is that they are, for one reason or another, so overwhelmed by their inner struggles with depression and insecurity that the illusory and transient "relief" of their addiction is more important than anything else.

Alcoholism: The Case History of a Friend

About eight years ago I noticed that a friend of mine was drinking heavily. He was obviously on a course toward self-destruction. I conveyed to Chris that the relationship we had was very important to me. I told him, "I need your friendship. Where will I ever find someone like you?" I recalled for him all the wonderful memories, rituals, and traditions we shared. Because I cared for him, I also kept a written record of all the times he didn't keep appointments, lied, and broke promises to me. When the time seemed right, I confronted Chris with it. I focused on my own disappointment rather than attacking him. I gave up suggesting he seek help (after investigating possible programs and offering the results to Chris). He had steadfastly refused all efforts in this direction. Chris made me promise, as a condition of our ongoing friendship, that I wouldn't mention it again. I agreed, with the proviso that if at some time in the future I felt he might be receptive, I could bring it up again. He agreed. All the while our friendship remained intact. We went out together (without our wives) two or three times a month. We spoke on the phone at least once a week. We also went out as two couples at least twice a month. Although Chris drank when we were out together, I never saw him in a state of intoxication. He drank in secret, or at a favorite bar. In the meantime I was getting frantic calls from his wife, who was reporting all the signs of the alcoholic, which I enumerated above. Chris's job, as a high-level executive in the computer field, was threatened.

Though this may sound surprising, I never suggested AA to Chris. He was a confirmed atheist, and I knew he would not be receptive to some of the spiritual messages in the AA program. Although AA is very good for many, I was sure he would not find it a sympathetic group. I mention this as a precaution. Giving the wrong advice—and having a friend follow it—could make it much harder for the person in trouble to get the help he or she needs later.

Keep in mind, however, that it's not enough to tell a troubled friend to "get help." True caring requires a bit of legwork. If you have a problem pal similar to mine, find out about the resources available to you. This book will give you a start.

Sometimes I would ask Chris in an offhand way, "Do you know the source of your resentment and anger?" (Incidentally, neither of his parents was alcoholic.) Sometimes he would talk a little. He'd get so depressed, however, that I knew he'd leave me and go off to his favorite bar if I pushed the conversation in the direction of his drinking. *By not trying to be his therapist, I was able to remain his friend.* For a while, we were still able to have a good time together.

The turning point came one evening when we went out together. Chris began some serious drinking. Almost before I knew what was happening, he began to open up to me in a way he had not done previously. He revealed a dramatic and deeply personal account of abuse by his father. Suddenly Chris's anguished fear that he could never measure up to his father (a complex inferiority struggle) emerged, as did his guilt about what his alcoholism was doing to his wife and children.

A common story? Maybe. But the point is that, by keeping a line of communication open between us, I was able to be there for Chris when he was ready to make a change for the better. He was making his first big move to get out from under a terrible weight, and I was also getting something I'd wanted for a long time: the potential to have my friend back on a healthier road, with the promise of many more good times for us ahead. We hugged and cried together. Chris agreed to enter a rehabilitation hospital.

Unfortunately, the story doesn't end happily there. The twenty-eight-day rehab program proved unsuccessful, and Chris resumed drinking after three months. The prescribed AA follow-through program seemed to make matters worse. Don't misunderstand me: AA is one of the best programs available, but like most programs it works only as well as the motivation of the participants. Yet relative to other programs it has one of the highest percentages of success.

In fact, most rehab programs for addicts do not work. Relapse rates tend to range from 50 to 75 percent. I have found that most after-care programs—even in AA—do not deal adequately with relationships. Friends and relatives often don't realize that the most important work needs to be done *after* the so-called completion of a program.

One year later, a secular-based outpatient therapy program proved successful for Chris. As of this date, he has been sober for six years because he dealt effectively with the problems that pushed him into using alcohol as a "remedy."

As most of us already realize, it's time for attitudes to change regarding the thoughtless encouraging of friends to drink. Perhaps it's best to start by entertaining in different ways. Offer guests nonalcoholic beverages when they visit. On the other hand, you do not have to refrain from serving alcohol just because a guest is an alcoholic. *Alcoholics are responsible for their own behavior in private and social situations.* If you are serving lunch or dinner, a glass or two of wine is a nice accompaniment to the meal, but alcohol should never be the focal point or purpose of a gathering. One further note of caution: If you are entertaining a person you know is an alcoholic, do not serve any food prepared with alcohol. There is no guarantee that all the alcohol will evaporate during the cooking process. This is poison for an alcoholic and may trigger a return to drinking. The chemistry of alcohol dependency can be physical, psychological, or a combination of both. Surely you would not want to risk your friend's sobriety by serving a dish prepared with alcohol. Just as it is now an accepted practice not to allow smoking in one's home, it is equally acceptable not to serve, encourage, or "push" alcoholic drinks or "recreational drugs."

Sobriety Is a Process

Staying sober is very different from "getting sober." People detoxify in a controlled setting, which can be of their own creation or institutional. Once sober, they cannot count on feeling so healthy that they will not want to drink or take drugs again. Staying sober takes a daily, sometimes hourly, pledge to continue on *without* their drug of choice. As long as everything else in the addict's life is going along well, the vow to stay sober is easier to maintain. If there is additional stress, such as problems with relationships or jobs, the "easy way out" is effortless and becomes *very* tempting. Many people will "fall off the wagon," but that does not mean that they take their sobriety lightly. Most of these people try again and again until they get it right—even if it takes thirty times! As long as alcoholics and drug addicts return for help and support, they are serious about living healthy lives. They have not given up on themselves—and we should not give up on them. (Very often we put addicts down when they "use their drug," but we forget to tell them how truly strong they are when they resume a sober life-style—which takes a great deal of courage for them.)

Think of it this way: Sobriety is a process, as well as a learned behavior. If someone starts drinking or using again it does not necessarily mean failure but rather an *interruption* of the process. What we always hope is that a breakthrough will occur that will allow the addict to be released from pain. This pain is what pulls an addict back into self-destructive behavior. If we truly care, we will help, encourage, and love our relative or friend by supporting the person—not the addictive behavior—for as long as it takes.

Here are some ideas to consider:

- Don't expect promises to be kept; don't believe lies.
- Don't let an alcoholic outsmart you or involve you as an accomplice in the evasion of responsibility.
- Learn everything you can about the effects of alcohol and particular drugs.
- Learn to spot the symptoms of use and withdrawal. Become a drug and alcohol expert.
- Believe that alcoholism and drug abuse are progressive illnesses and will always get worse if not treated.
- Join a support group for relatives of abusers. Learn as much as you can about substance abuse and how to handle your personal interactions with an abuser. Do this for yourself!

Research all the local drug- and alcohol-abuse programs you can. Talk to staff; understand their philosophy, forms of care, and lengths of treatment. What do they recommend as follow-up care? If "your" addict is an adult, does he or she have insurance that will cover this treatment? If not, are you able and willing to take on some of the cost of care? Are any public assistance programs available? Is there a waiting list? Are there other resources that might be of help? Your church or synagogue? Live-and-work programs? Rich relatives or friends? (I don't mean to sound flippant about this, but a good program of care may actually require the assets of someone else who truly cares.) Learn *everything* you possibly can.

If your local programs are either sparse or inadequate, look beyond your city or town. Investigate county and state resources; go national if you must. Private hospitals and rehabilitation centers should not be ignored, even if you know you can't afford them. They will still give you information about treatment and refer you to other facilities within their network. The staff of a private hospital that is part of a national chain can provide you with a list of other institutions they own, which in turn will give you the names of people to call in other cities. They all "know the competition" in their communities. You will learn a lot about various treatment programs, especially if the public relations personnel think you might provide them with a "paying customer." Incidentally, I'm not being critical here. In fact, I would like it if public facilities and the "not for profit" institutions had this same "we're the best" attitude about their programs and their ability to help their client.

Make it personal! Get to know—at the very least, via telephone—the people who deal with these problems daily.

Intervention: Training Yourself for Effective Action

When the problem of any addiction (whether it's substance abuse, gambling, eating, etc.) becomes critical or there is evidence that the addict is out of control, you now have the information that will help the abuser to decide what form of treatment to take. Best of all, you will have used your energy in a positive way. Rather than allowing yourself to become debilitated by anger, anxiety, and consternation, you will have trained yourself for action. Such self-empowerment prepares you to help, even if the person is not yet ready to accept treatment.

In the beginning of this book I told the story about a friend's daughter who had become a heroin addict and how a friend convinced her to call home for help. To continue that story here, I would like to relate how the family intervened and got the daughter into a rehabilitation center. (Although this young woman was willing, the process would have been the same even if an angry confrontation had been necessary.) The family gathered all available members—an aunt, an uncle, cousins, and siblings. They shared their shock at learning what had happened and began to brainstorm possible actions that might be necessary. The young woman told her family what she was facing in terms of withdrawal. Doctors and pharmacists were consulted so everyone could understand the process and respond to her pain in the most appropriate manner.

Next, because they were unprepared for the situation, they called several hospitals to find out about rehabilitation programs. A joint decision was made about which hospital she would go to, but the hospital could not take her for four days. They planned how they would stay with her during the next four days. They discussed with her the fact that because she had admitted this problem, there was no way for her to return to her former life. It just wouldn't happen. (Understanding how very vulnerable she was to her peers' opinions and direction made this necessary. Stronger-willed persons could learn not to take drugs and stay within familiar surroundings.) She didn't object, because she was starting to withdraw from the drug and had no physical strength. She could not think clearly because of what was happening to her body.

The family told her that if she left home for drugs (which she threatened to do), someone would find her and bring her back. They emphasized to her that she was not going to be released from the arms of love *ever*. If she relapsed—tomorrow or ten years from now—she would *never* be deserted. She actually wanted to get well and so agreed to go along with all joint decisions. During the time before she went to the hospital, her things were removed from the apartment she shared with her boyfriend and another roommate. She was given nourishing food, rest, massage, over-the-counter medications (according to a drug counselor's and pharmacist's instructions), and lots of understanding until she went to the hospital. It was two weeks before she began to understand the direction her life had taken. Her personal resolve to *stay* well began at this time.

You have not read about any anger here. I am told there was a great deal of anger (on everyone's part), but it was saved for an appropriate time and place. As part of the hospital's program there was a controlled situation with counselors present where issues—from old family business to the effects of the addiction on family members—were dealt with. Deep feelings surface in exercises like this and can be the beginning of lifesaving honesty. My friend said that regardless of how wrenching these exercises are, they offer an occasion for a breakthrough and a new opportunity for genuine communication.

This intervention, while longer than some, is not unusual given the lack of sufficient rehabilitation facilities, even for those able to pay for them. So back to the original point: If you are aware of an abuse problem, *learn as much as you can about available resources*. You never know when the right time for intervention and the beginning of recovery will come. There is no reason why friends rather than family couldn't do exactly the same thing for someone they love. Good timing plus caring are necessary requirements for such an action.

CHAPTER 9

❦

Families with a Disabled Child or Adult

Only when our empathy is based on some knowledge and an awareness of how hard it is to take care of someone who is permanently disabled—unable to survive without support—can we play a significant role in improving the quality of our friend's life and that of the child. Don't mind your own business; be a source of comfort and help. I am taking a different approach here by giving advice directly to the parents whose children are disabled. By reviewing my suggestions, you as a friend could have a better understanding of the dilemmas involved. (If you want more details on the subject of disabilities, please see *One Miracle at a Time* by Irving Dickman with Sol Gordon.)

For the Parents

Be aware of the inalienable rights of parents of children with disabilities. The first right—which, like all the others is allowable, valid, and sane—is to mourn, to feel sorry for yourself, and to agonize over the question "Why me?" The right to work through all of the could'ves and should'ves in your life is also reasonable. Admissible, too, are death wishes. Blame or praise God, or question why He has forsaken you.

And then—as soon as possible for you—come to the conclusion that you will never know the answers to most of your important questions. If the question "Why me?" eventually becomes "Why *not* me?" then you are ready to deal actively with self-pity, denial, anger, and whatever other emotions you might be feeling. Furthermore, you now realize you have to do the best you can and get on with your life.

Your life hasn't been made less worthwhile because you have a severely disabled child. In fact, you have the right to feel that you are not only doing the best you can but also that you are coping with an enormously difficult situation with all the information and understanding you have at this time.

Along with your right to feel you are doing the best you can comes an enormous responsibility: It is essential not to judge anyone else on the basis of your *own* expectations. Your spouse, for example, may be doing the best he or she can simply by returning to everyday routines—work, for example. A sibling or an older, healthy child in your family might not be anywhere near meeting your expectations or requirements.

By being a model and an inspiration, you can accomplish a great deal. By being a nag, by wallowing in self-pity, or by being preoccupied with the tragedy, you will undermine all of the things you need to accomplish.

You have the right to begin organizing your life selfishly, to your own satisfaction. More than ever you need hobbies, distractions, excitements. At no previous time did you need opportunities for leisure and pleasure as much as you do now. Do the things you enjoy, even if you feel you can't afford the time or the money and even if you feel your neighbors will misinterpret what you do.

Friends, especially, should take note of the above paragraph. This is no time for them to be minding their own business!

The final right is absolutely essential: Allow yourself to have a sense of humor. Family life can become grim with everyone walking on eggshells, and laughter can be misunderstood at these times. Yet nobody can survive a tragic situation without laughter.

I shall never forget the story of a fifteen-year-old boy with a learning disability who was asked by his mother to take out the garbage. His response was, "I can't take out the garbage—I'm brain-injured." His mother replied, "If you don't want to be brain-injured twice, you had better take out the garbage." This incident happened in a lively, active home where people were more than just survivors. They lived a good, full life.

You get no points for being the parent of a child with a disability. For you, everything in life is harder, and in every sense—emotionally and financially—more costly. Comfort or peace of mind will not come from comparing yourself with anyone else, even if you know objectively that many other people's troubles are worse than yours.

The biggest problems develop when the whole family becomes disorganized around the existence, care, and management of a disabled child. That problem is magnified, of course, when there is more than one disabled child in a family. However, families can organize and support each other, especially in situations where (1) once-unified families are threatened with breakdown, and (2) families are hanging together because of determination and commitment but lack the previous sparkle, spontaneity, and joy of family life.

Here are a few suggestions intended to enhance your strength in dealing with a disabled child and your family. Recognize that the hardest thing to recover from is anger. Yet anger diluted with forgiveness has a special alchemy—it becomes determination, if not courage, to do the best you can. Accepting your anger without guilt helps to reorganize your family. It can also put your own life into orbit by giving priority to yourself, no matter how much you need to attend to your spouse and children. More than anything else, and no matter how miserable you still feel, *do not isolate yourself*.

The best test of whether you are working in the right direction is the amount of energy you have. Discounting extreme situations (recovering from an accident, etc.), *energy is mainly a psychological phenomenon*. How often have you experienced a period of exhaustion that instantly turns into boundless energy upon meeting someone you care about, or upon receiving an unexpected surprise visit or phone call, or upon learning something new?

Haven't you also noticed that mature love experiences are energizing, while immature ones are exhausting? If you are working toward maximizing autonomy for your child, if you believe that your past is not your potential, if you have some faith or optimism, and if you are determined to consider the needs of the whole family, you do not have to accomplish very much before you notice that you have a great deal of energy.

Remember that unhappiness itself is alienating, because people shun those who are unhappy. It's really a two-way street, however, since people who are miserable often resent other people's happiness. Be aware of these feelings in yourself. They can be conquered. Your reassurance and confidence about your marriage and family may have been threatened, but knowing that the odds are against you makes it even more important to do the best you can and get on with your life.

Here are some parental rights and insights:

1. You don't have to devote your entire life to the "cause." You are free to devote as much as you want or to get away from it for a while.
2. You need freedom to take your time in deciding what to do. You have the right to shop around for competent professional help. You have the right not to accept advice or even comfort, especially from people who say things such as, "You think you have troubles?"
3. It is all right to intervene, to arrange parties, and to rendezvous with friends on behalf of your child.
4. It's all right to consider institutionalization, even if it goes against the current trend toward home care.
5. You have the right to feel that it is not God's will, nor is it a punishment.
6. You have the right to feel that it is God's will. (But then you still have to figure out what His will means to you: Does it mean that He would not have given you and your family such a chal-

lenge if He didn't think you were strong enough to handle it?)

7. It is your right to consider sending your child to a camp for the summer, even if the child does not want to go. It is amazing how most children end up having a really good experience.

8. You are entitled to good and bad moods. You have the right not to be perfect—even to have hostile thoughts—and the right *not* to *act* on such thoughts for your own well-being and that of your family. It's all right to feel bad and mourn from time to time.

9. Consider becoming an expert in the disability you are concerned about—even if your motive is initially to help your own child.

10. Don't neglect the comfort your religion can provide.

11. Expect your child to learn to live fully within the family. You can get help to accomplish this.

12. Show by example the need to joke, fool around, and be silly. That's a safety valve for everyone in the family!

13. Consider finding out how to get some use out of all the sorrow, whether it is through writing poetry, painting, or understanding the needs of other people in a more sensitive and compassionate way. Use your tragedy and sorrow constructively, or it will use you. It can be done!

14. Become a health nut. Teach children how to develop healthy life-styles.

15. Use your experiences to be helpful to other parents.

16. Be proud of your accomplishments.
17. There is a powerful need for parents to be on their own, to get away from everything by going on vacations—or just generally doing things—without their children. No healthy, mature family functions well in a posture of constant togetherness.
18. Plan times that are special for the brothers and sisters of the disabled child. Without these breaks, siblings are more likely to resent their responsibilities to their disabled brother or sister.
19. You have a right to expect miracles. Why operate on the assumption that our current scope of knowledge is a verdict of doom?

Let me say to all of you brave—and often lonely—families out there that if a friend asks you "Is there anything I can do?" always, and I mean *always*, say yes. Give your friend a small task to do. *Sometimes we lose friends during a crisis because they are confused and uncertain about what is expected of them.* Give old friends a chance to prove their reliability, and allow friends-in-the-making an opportunity to become more firmly bonded with you. (And to those of you who have friends with a disabled child, reverse the following requests for help into offerings. Show your desire to be involved in their lives.)

- Could you spare two hours a week and stay with _____ so I can go shopping?
- Would you call once a week? I so enjoy chatting with you.
- Would you send notes and articles you think would

be of interest to _____? Items of interest add fuel to our conversations.

• When you go to the movies, would you invite us to go with you once in a while? Incidentally, we pay our own way.

Couldn't you think of many more tasks for friends to do? Maybe you will lose most of your friends by being so bold as to suggest specific ways that they can help, but face it: You were in the process of losing them anyway. Soon you'll find out who your true friends are! If you don't find out this way —*your* way—you might end up angry, bitter, and very much alone. Not only that, but you could also miss out on opportunities to meet the needs of friends, new and old, who truly *do* want to be helpful.

I think it is important for friends to understand what the parents of a handicapped child can reasonably expect. For those who have never been close to such a situation, it is important to raise your sensitivity level. Sympathy is *not* what is needed. What is needed is for you to become a force for constructive help. As a friend you have the power to increase the confidence the family needs to deal with their situation. The professionals—therapists, teachers, indeed, all those who are part of the care team—will reflect their views and feelings on the family and thereby directly influence the integration and acceptance of the special condition into daily life.

As a friend, show that you are ready to do practical tasks. Any time you free your friend to take a break, you are helping. Remember to talk about your activities and share the sad and the happy moments in your own life; keep all aspects of your relationship alive.

Nat and Bess lost many of their good, long-standing (from childhood) friends after their adult daughter Janice emerged from a tragic boating accident as a quadriplegic. At a time when they desperately needed emotional and financial help, very little of it was forthcoming. (To this day I feel guilty that I did so little to help, but in subsequent years I tried to compensate for this—not out of guilt, I believe, but out of love.)

Janice says that she still feels hurt that many of her friends, including those who were on the boat with her at the time of the accident, found it "impossible" to visit her. As a tribute to this courageous family, who are my cousins, I want to share an essay written by Janice's parents a couple of years after her accident in 1980.

What Do You Say to a Quad?

One of the saddest by-products of a catastrophic illness or injury is the departure of friends, even of family.

"There are a million people out there who are hurting, and in despair," writes Rabbi Harold Kushner in the best-seller *When Bad Things Happen to Good People*. They need your help.

Heaped upon the trauma of a debilitating illness is the defection of oh-so-many friends and acquaintances who "cannot take your sadness."

Our daughter was injured two and a half years ago in a motor boat accident. Her scalp was torn, her neck broken with two vertebrae fractured. She recovered from all. But her spinal cord was injured too, and that, we are told, is permanent. She is a C5–C6 quadriplegic, unable to move her hands or legs, unable to control personal body functions.

At the time of her injury, Janice was at her peak. She had a good job, was a junior at college pursuing a business degree, an amateur actress who had appeared in eight shows in three years, a member of several amateur theatrical groups, and had plenty of dates.

Janice spent seven months in a hospital and rehab center, fighting and hopeful every minute. Her sense of humor sparkled. "What can I do for you today?" asked her doctor. "Get me a body transplant," she would say.

"I had dozens of people outside my room waiting to see me. There were hundreds of cards and letters on the walls. What happened to everybody?"

Today Janice has the love, companionship, and care of her immediate family. Depression surrounds not only her, but her family. What is sadly absent are signs of support, acts of love from the many who are still around, but who cannot cope with our tragedy.

Dr. Leo Buscaglia, in his book *Living, Loving and Learning*, urges us to touch somebody, to hug somebody, to get on the phone, drop a card. Love is so important, he says, not only for the recipient, but for the giver.

What would it take to write an occasional letter, to make a once-a-month call, even to drop in if you're in the neighborhood? It is tragic enough to awake each morning unable to get out of bed without the help of an aide. You're dependent on aides to take a shower, get dressed, have food prepared so you can eat it. But then comes the prospect of another empty day, with

TV or reading to make the time go by, but with over-whelming loneliness to add to your burden.

Quads are courageous. They fight to exist. That humorist-columnist, Erma Bombeck, once wrote that if there was a Ten Best list for courage, she would vote for paralyzed people for all ten spots. Imagine the guts you need to be dragged out of bed, to depend on others for your basic health needs, and to cope with the cruel truth that that's how it's going to be for the rest of your life.

Our Janice is a heroic fighter. She is driven to work three days a week as a receptionist and switchboard operator. She uses a special headset and punches the buttons with a pencil that is inserted into a cuff around her wrist. Four hours a day is all she can handle, but she "loves it." She says it's her "window on the world."

We know it is hard to sit with a person who is paralyzed, or who has a terminal illness, or in whose family some tragedy has occurred. But after that visit, *you* walk away. You may feel bad, you may even throw up afterward. But you will have given some aid and comfort to one who hungers for it. That goes not only for the ailing one, but for the family as well.

We who have reached adulthood have thousands of memories. We've had a hundred friends. We shared interests and activities, went to shows and dinners together, discussed books, politics, the news. In many cases, our basic roots were intertwined. Is this the end —one abandons the tragic family, a family already reeling from the enormous catastrophe that so suddenly struck our lives?

Rabbi Kushner, Dr. Buscaglia, even Erma Bombeck would say, and so do we, "Come sit. Hold our hand. Listen to our grief with patience. Talk about your own experiences. But let us know we're not abandoned." People need people. Even if you say nothing, your very presence is eloquent.

If you drop that note or make that call every now and then, it will help us carry the burden, and who knows? It might even make you feel better too.

What do you say to a quad? Say "Hello."

Everyone's Suffering Is Unique: The Fine Art of Listening Well

Before I leave this subject, let me mention one of the pitfalls people often face in dealing with a friend's disabled or handicapped family member. There's a tendency for people unwittingly to judge the degree of distress felt in particular circumstances. At their best, nonjudgmental friends can make us feel special, wanted, and capable of overcoming whatever troubles life throws our way.

However, unless we feel an urgent need to jolt a friend out of dwelling or wallowing in static, destructive self-pity, it's best to listen sympathetically to what they say. In fact, my experience has been that most people just want a friend's ear so they can share a deeper sense of what their life has been like. Chances are your friend will *not* be looking for pity. He or she may be trying to say, "The difficulties I have faced—and continue to face—are as meaningful to me as my joys. They make my life special in many ways."

Let me be more specific. No friend who confides in us

about his or her handicapped child (or, for that matter, who shares any distress or suffering) wants to hear that we know of someone *else* who has a child even *more* severely handicapped. In one instance I was with a group of friends when one opened up about what it was like to bring up his severely handicapped child. An otherwise intelligent, sensitive, and caring older woman responded by telling of a neighbor who had to bring up *three* children who were severely disabled.

Such responses usually distance a friend's personal life by making it more general and abstract, which is exactly what is *not* wanted by someone who confides his or her story to us. Of course, the example cited above is not sympathetic listening, nor is it anything approaching empathy for a friend's unique situation.

When a friend tells of his plight, no matter what it may be, it's never a good idea to top it. No one's suffering should be spoken of in the context of a competitive sport. If you do not know what to say, it is best to remain silent.

In another case, a friend with an older brother who suffered brain damage early in life and was never able to talk told me how disheartened he was after finally being able to talk to a friend about his feelings about his brother. This particular friend's response was to leap into a story about people he knew who had a *violently* handicapped child. "At least your brother was gentle," he said. "These parents had to deal with heavy guilt feelings caused by the physical punishment their child meted out to them daily!" The impact of this response was to trivialize his friend's anguish.

What would you say to such a reply? My friend told me he went back into his shell of silence about his brother. Better, he told me, not to speak of him at all, since his brother's handicap was too easily seen as nothing special in the larger scheme of things. He also began to feel as though the twenty years he spent as one of his brother's primary caretakers did not really amount to much. Of course, it amounts to a great deal, and a friend could have helped him see that.

The examples cited above reveal a crucial dimension of friendship: listening skills. This talent and sensitivity are open to everyone. Listening well is almost like an art form because it takes a lifetime to develop and grow. Where the growth of friendship is concerned, listening becomes an act of attention with as much power as the sun. Indeed, when asked, most people said they felt closest to those friends who made the effort to listen well and understand.

No one can tell how a child will deal with his or her handicap as they get older. Your friend will hear all kinds of things about his or her child from other parents, brothers, sisters, friends, teachers, therapists, and doctors. Yet the important thing to remember, as the journalist and photographer Jill Krementz discovered in her marvelous book *How It Feels to Live with a Physical Disability*, is, "Above all, they do not feel sorry for themselves, and they do not want us to feel sorry for them either."

In her book, Ms. Krementz lets the children—ages six to sixteen and living with blindness, paralysis, birth anomalies, and other disabilities—describe, in their own words, what their lives are like. "I prefer to think of the young people who tell their stories as merely different," the author writes in her introduction, "as diverse in their individual ways as we all are."

This brings up another important point: We all need to be reminded how strong a child can become with the nourishment of family love and caring friends. As Helen Keller once noted, "A person who is severely impaired never knows his hidden sources of strength until he is treated like a normal human being and encouraged to shape his own life."

As Cheri Register has observed in her book *Living with Chronic Illness*, "Friends . . . are the ones who can still see and affirm the healthy aspects of our personalities despite the overlay of illness [or tragedy], who recognize our need for diversion and normalcy and are not afraid of humor in the face of tragedy. Yet, they also respect our right to solitude, when that is what serves us best."

It is important to remember that caretakers who maintain their sense of humor are more likely to keep their friends than those who take on the role of a martyr. *Both* sides need to keep an oppressive sense of obligation out of the friendship.

Register, whose work reflects her own experience as one of the (as she puts it) "interminably ill," has also noted, "The kind of friendship that can be maintained 'in sickness and in health' . . . requires genuine empathy, an ability to see you as an individual, not just a sick [or victimized] person. Rather than merely giving, sincere friends give on terms appropriate to your unique character. In short, they get to know *you*."

But the reverse is also true: Caring people who are dealing with a tragedy must try to ask for help within the limits of their friends' capabilities. Some friends can give a lot, some a little, depending on *their* circumstances. It is difficult to recognize this truth if we are asking too much or continually projecting anger and frustration about our tragedy onto those who might otherwise be willing to help us.

People fare much better when they know what it takes to keep friends coming to see them and being helpful. John, a quadriplegic now in his sixties, remains cheerful and always ready to hear and tell jokes. He is always kidding around, has lots of friends, and people enjoy their visits with him. Another man I know is a hemophiliac and far less disabled than John. Still, he is mostly depressed and usually agonizes over his fate, asking, "Why me?" and "Why this disease?" Good questions. However, no one wants to hear them over and over. Now he has no visitors, and his biggest complaint is that his friends have abandoned him. His behavior was so obnoxious that he literally threw his friends out. I am ashamed to admit that I, too, have rejected him, and we are no longer friends. Writing this book is forcing me to consider a reconciliation and make another effort—if only I can be a big enough person to tolerate his despair and help him overcome it. Sometimes it's a two-way street.

We may expect friendship to be like a flag in our time of great need, but not all of our friends may be able to rally around it immediately. Don't cut them off. Given some time, they may eventually be able to respond and come back to the relationship. It is never clear why some people are not there for us when we need them. Don't judge their situation—it is not always possible for you to know the circumstances that prevent people from responding as we wish they would.

CHAPTER 10

❧

Depression and Suicide

The extreme sadness of a young person is often overlooked by parents, and sometimes it creeps up on the family without any particular advance notice. What I would like to do here is not only alert parents to the possibility of a depressed son or daughter, but also suggest that the objective eye of a good friend might be a saving grace. I include this in the hope of alerting just one family or just one young person who might come to the aid of a friend. Being depressed for a short time is not the same as chronic depression that lasts months or (without help) even years. But it doesn't matter which kind it is; the sooner it is recognized and treated, the better.

Recognizing Depression—for Your Friend's Sake

Those who see one or more of the following symptoms in someone they know and care about should be especially alert, since these can indicate substance abuse, depression, or both. Understand this: The person is in trouble and needs help. The symptoms are:

- Frequently expressed feelings of sadness, emptiness, worthlessness, shame, hopelessness, and/or helplessness
- Inability to concentrate, or indecisiveness
- Persistent loss of appetite
- Complaints of memory loss
- Feeling tired a lot
- Decline in school or work achievement
- Increase in moodiness
- Change in sleep behavior
- Worsening personal hygiene
- Moping around, excessive "sighing" for no apparent reason
- Withdrawal from family activities
- Withdrawal from friends or taking on "new" friends whom they don't want us to know

About 10 percent of teenagers suffer from serious periods of depression. That's about 1.5 million people under 20 years of age. About 30,000 people commit suicide in the United States every year, including some 5,000 people under 24 years of age. Perhaps the numbers don't seem large, but note that about a million people *attempt* suicide every year. All of the above symptoms occur in adults as well. Many illnesses are much more difficult to overcome when depression is involved.

The National Mental Health Association estimates that, overall, more than 18 million adults suffer from serious depression at some time in any one year and that some two-thirds of those suffering from depression will not seek treatment. Most are reluctant to do so because the disease is widely perceived to be a personal flaw rather than a health problem. Depression among older Americans is a major public health crisis.

The most important message here is that depression is an eminently treatable disorder. If someone you care about is depressed, seek medical help and at the same time read a very clear and sensible book titled *Depression: What Families Should Know*, by Elaine Fantle-Shimberg. I would also read William Styron's *Darkness Visible: A Memoir of Madness*, which is a remarkable autobiographical vision of a recovery from severe depression.

Here we should note that I am not talking about periods of sadness or depressed feelings related to tragic situations. The depression I speak of appears to be without apparent cause, although it is often precipitated by an illness. It is also long-lasting and often has devastating consequences.

Suicide: An Avoidable Consequence of Depression

We know that all suicide attempts are cries for help. Most adults who commit suicide do so after prolonged periods of depression, but young people are more likely to act impulsively or in anger. The emotion underlying virtually all attempts to kill oneself is a feeling of *hopelessness*.

Although depression, despair, feelings of emptiness, and hopelessness are key factors in suicide, the lack of internal resources and energy to cope with disappointment are also factors in most impulsive suicides. Reasons are often related to the end of a love affair, fears of homosexuality, the death of a loved one, or a failure to achieve an important goal (such as acceptance to a particular college). Alcohol or drug use can facilitate a suicide attempt, as can a bitter argument with a parent or girlfriend or boyfriend.

Recent findings in the field of suicide prevention reveal new factors, besides depression, as contributing to suicide and suicide attempts. The unresolved death of someone close and the fear of being "found out" after a serious mistake is made—a pregnancy, a brush with the law (especially in families where communication is not open)—are now considered serious risk factors. It is difficult to know what will be a risk for particular individuals, because seldom do seriously troubled persons talk freely about what is preying on their minds. More and more evidence indicates that the ready availability of a gun in the home greatly multiplies the chances of a suicide.

It has become very clear to me as I've studied many suicides among adolescents and young adults that pointing the finger of responsibility at parents (or others) is rarely appropriate. Parents may be an influence, but I've rarely seen a case where I could comfortably suggest that parents should be held accountable. Sometimes the "worst" that can be said is that parents and others close to the person were not alert enough to the signs of trouble. But we don't live in a society that prepares us to be wary of such a possibility, *especially* among those we know best. Ironic, isn't it? Still, adults do have control over the availability of firearms within the home. They can learn healthy communication skills, learn to recognize depression, and can teach coping skills to their children.

Experts in the field agree that, in addition to symptoms

of depression, there are some suicide risk signs that warrant *immediate* attention, including medical and psychiatric intervention:

- Talk of death and talk of suicide (even if objectively stated, this is an "alert")
- Saying, "I won't be missed," or "Everybody will be better off without me," or "You won't have to worry about me much longer"
- Giving previously treasured possessions away (clothing, jewelry, tapes/discs, hobby or sports equipment, etc.)
- Taking saved money and spending it or giving it away
- Trying *new*, risky, or daring behaviors, especially if not previously interested

Everyone should be on special alert if there is a sense of hopelessness, irrational thinking, or prolonged sadness after a broken love affair, the death of a close friend or relative, or a previous suicide attempt.

Please read the following special appeal from a bereaved mother. She writes:

Please Promise Me that You Won't Do Anything to Hurt Yourself

I spoke with one of the leading suicide researchers in the country about two weeks before my son decided to take his own life. He told me that the most important intervention for a severely depressed person was to get them to promise not to do anything to hurt themselves. I didn't use that intervention with my son because I was totally unaware that he might become suicidal. So that my son may not have totally died in vain, I am asking YOU to please promise me that YOU won't do anything to hurt yourself. It is depression that is distorting your thinking. My son wrote that he was stupid, at a time when he was being elected to Phi Beta Kappa. My son said he was lonely, that he had alienated almost everyone. My son was revered by many. Depression brings distorted thinking.

My son was a kind, concerned, and thoughtful person. I can't believe that he would have wanted to contribute so much pain to so many people. He wouldn't have wanted to spoil graduation for his housemates or his girlfriend. My son said he felt guilty about the cost of his education and the sacrifice that it entailed. Not graduating, not fulfilling any promise after graduation was certainly not a rational solution to irrational guilt. I'm sure my son would not have wanted any one of thousands of ordinary situations to cause me remorse and pain, searing, sharp, horrid pain. I'm sure that my son would not have wanted to destroy elderly and sick grandparents. My son made a grievous error. You can make a better choice. PLEASE, PLEASE PROMISE ME THAT YOU WON'T DO ANYTHING TO HURT YOURSELF OR ANYONE ELSE BY RASH IMPULSE OR DIS-TORTED THOUGHT. If I sound desperate, I am. I can't imagine that my sensitive, accomplished son would have wanted to harm his friends and family.

Help and relief will eventually come. A friend of

my son had a major depression. She tried to hurt herself, and failed. She got treatment. She is now well. It might take time, but you will get well too. In the meantime, your promising not to hurt yourself is the only consolation I can have. Please, help to console me. Promise that if you have out-of-control feelings, you'll call 911, or call a hospital. Right now, find someone to call, and write that number down. Put it where you can easily find it at any time. I know the world is full of answering machines. But if you plan now you can help to save yourself if the need arises. Remember, I am counting on it. Thank you.

Vigilance is in order here. While I believe it's an excellent idea to get a commitment that the person will not commit suicide, it should not be considered a rationalization for avoiding all the other precautions, including medical and psychological help and even hospitalization, that often must be taken. I know from personal sadness that you can't count on a commitment, although I emphasize again that it's a good part of the strategy.

One clear message has emerged from the experiences of people who have had to cope with the trauma of the violent death of loved ones either from accident, murder, or suicide. Those who seem to have been able to lessen the pain to manageable levels have been able to devote themselves to organizations related to the trauma (such as work with the Victims of Violent Crimes).

Thoughts of such an event—the suicide of a loved one —are so unbearable to me that I'm truly unable to express myself well enough to be helpful to others. So allow me to turn to my friend Iris Bolton for help. She, like the woman who wrote the above letter, lost a son to suicide. In her long, hard road to recovery, she has become one of America's preeminent teachers in helping survivors endure. Her book *My Son . . . My Son: A Guide to Healing After Death, Loss, or Suicide* is especially valuable.

The following is her advice. Friends of survivors would do well to read it over carefully to be helpful in easing pain.

Beyond Surviving: Suggestions for Survivors, by Iris M. Bolton

Hundreds of books have been written about loss and grief. Few have addressed the aftermath of suicide for survivors. Here again, there are no answers; only suggestions from those who have lived through and beyond the event. I've compiled their thoughts.

1. Know you can survive. You may not think so, but you can.
2. Struggle with "why" it happened until you no longer need to know "why" or until you are satisfied with partial answers.
3. Know you may feel overwhelmed by the intensity of your feelings but all your feelings are normal.
4. Anger, guilt, confusion, forgetfulness are common responses. You are not crazy; you are in mourning.
5. Be aware you may feel appropriate anger at the person, at the world, at God, at yourself. It's okay to express it.
6. You may feel guilty for what you think you did or

did not do. Guilt can turn into regret, through forgiveness.

7. Having suicidal thoughts is common. It does not mean that you will act on those thoughts.

8. Remember to take one moment or one day at a time.

9. Find a good listener with whom to share. Call someone if you need to talk.

10. Don't be afraid to cry. Tears are healing.

11. Give yourself time to heal.

12. Remember, the choice was not yours. No one is the sole influence in another's life.

13. Expect setbacks. If emotions return like a tidal wave you may only be experiencing a remnant of grief, an unfinished piece.

14. Try to put off major decisions.

15. Give yourself permission to get professional help.

16. Be aware of the pain of your family and friends.

17. Be patient with yourself and with others who may not understand.

18. Set your own limits and learn to say no.

19. Steer clear of people who want to tell you what or how to feel.

20. Know that there are support groups that can be helpful, such as Compassionate Friends or Survivors of Suicide groups. If not, ask a professional to help start one.

21. Call on your personal faith to help you through.

22. It is common to experience physical reactions to your grief, e.g., headaches, loss of appetite, inability to sleep.

23. The willingness to laugh with others and at yourself is healing.
24. Wear out your questions, anger, guilt, or other feelings until you can let them go. Letting go doesn't mean forgetting.
25. Know that you will never be the same again, but you can survive and even go beyond just surviving.

CHAPTER 11

❦

Bereaved Parents:
When Hope Turns into Tragedy

Pregnancy is a time of intense expectation. The promise of new life gives everyone fresh hope: The next stage of a family life cycle is on its way. Your friends are going to be parents! Plans for the future suddenly take on an urgency they never had before. Even when a family has problems (financial, etc.) in their daily life, the anticipation of a new life diminishes the weight of these burdens.

When the birth occurs, most people report feelings of awe. Even those who claim not to be religious are likely to start speaking about the "miracle" of birth. But what happens when your friends' hopes and dreams are dashed by a stillbirth or a baby with severe physical and/or mental problems? Your friends may not yet know the cause or consequence of their tragedy, but one thing is sure. Pain, agony, confusion, and sensations of numbness have quickly replaced their feelings of joy.

When tragedy strikes, few words will offer comfort and none will remove the pain. Accepting that fact is the first step toward becoming a helpful friend.

Friends need to be a sounding board for grief. Be available to listen to the bereaved mother, father, other children, and grandparents. Although they will talk and cry among themselves, the bereaved family will also appreciate the times when they are able to speak freely with caring friends.

Infant Death

Every family deals with tragedy and grief in its own way. After losing a daughter during delivery, my friends John and Emily dealt with their grief in two distinct ways. For weeks after the death, Emily would go off alone and cry, but John found consolation talking with friends. The way parents need to express their grief will vary, depending on whether their case was one of premature delivery or problems in the fetal stage of pregnancy. Parents who want to hold their premature baby, or dress and rock it before letting the professionals take over, should be supported. So should the parents who choose to have the hospital dispose of a fetus, either after viewing it or without viewing it at all. Parental wishes come first.

Friends of mine who lost a baby two weeks after birth gave another dimension to the old saw about "speaking ill of the dead." The parents had pictures of their baby dressed for burial displayed in their living room after the baby died. (Because of all the medical equipment and critical care, they did not take pictures of the baby while he was alive.) The baby's grandmother thought this was "ghoulish" and "sick," and she wanted to forget the "whole incident!" Unfortunately, she felt compelled to judge and discourage the parents from mourning in their own way. Subsequent disagreements about what was "right" put a terrible strain on the grandmother's relationship with her son and daughter-in-law.

Why would parents want to do such a thing in the first place? First of all, the bereaved parents needed to remember that their baby did live, even if it was only for a short time. They lost a son who was part of them, but did not have a way to acknowledge that fact properly. They realized their feelings of loss would never go away completely. It was clear the pictures eased their pain by giving it a solid reality they could deal with rather than a vague, unexpressed power over them.

As Harriet Sarnoff Schiff wrote in her excellent, slim volume *The Bereaved Parent,* "The most essential ingredient . . . in surviving well—besides facing reality—is to speak of the dead child unashamedly." Some people, she noted, found such openness awkward, but most of them were grateful for the relief of not having to be guarded with their friends in speaking about their loss.

It should be noted also that in cases where the child was older, friends of the parents will have their own need to talk and grieve. After all, they knew the child too.

After the Loss: What to Expect and What to Do

Directly after the death of a baby, your friends' home will be in a confused state. Decision-making will be difficult at best. This is a time when a friend could do most of the preliminary inquiries relating to funeral and burial arrangements. In this way, you can help prepare the couple within their own more comfortable environment for what will be asked of them. This will give them time to understand the detailed actions they will have to take. Also, meetings with clergy or funeral directors will be given a chance to proceed more smoothly.

Looking In on the Mother in these Special Circumstances

The physical condition of the mother will be an overwhelming reminder of her loss. Her breasts may be full of milk. This, along with the postnatal healing process, will symbolize the awful reality she must face. Postpartum depression and the hormonal changes after childbirth can only serve to make matters worse for the woman *and* her husband. The grieving couple can share most of their sorrow. However, another woman might be able to understand more precisely how the physical symptoms affect the mother's emotions and feelings. A woman friend to hug and talk with would be especially helpful at this time.

Siblings Will Need Special Attention

When other children are present in your friends' family, there's a real need to maintain some semblance of normalcy. This means regular meals, baths, and bedtimes for the children.

Cooking, or even calling out for pizza, may prove too strenuous for the grieving parents. Indeed, without the help of family and friends, the problem could become serious.

The needs of small children can easily be overlooked during times of intense grief. They may not understand the change in family priorities, from them to a pervasive sadness they cannot comprehend. So if children are in the home, provide a supply of milk, fruit, bread, breakfast foods, and healthy treats. Make sure other friends and neighbors have been mobilized: They can bring prepared meals and staple foods on specific days.

Friends should keep in mind that coming into the home with a steady flow of meals or groceries for a few weeks will help take care of your friends, physically and emotionally. The parents will feel your support. Because there will be people coming in and out of the home, they will have an opportunity to talk about their loss if they choose to do so. In any case, it's a wonderful thing to do. *Nourishment* has a depth of meaning in this context.

Helping During the Hospital Period and After

Above all else, friends need to be available.

- Read about the loss of infants on your own. (Suggestions are given at the end of this book.)
- If you don't understand the family's beliefs about death, tell them you don't want to make any assumptions or mistakes. *Ask* if they will give you the name of someone who can help you understand.
- If the family wants to do something you do not believe to be correct (for whatever reason), respect

their wishes. Assist only if you feel comfortable, because your disapproval or tension will show.

- Offer to notify other friends for the parents. If their list is long, a telephone tree may help by dividing up the task among several people.

- If the parents require it, you can become a general contact person for them, explaining their wishes about visiting, funeral services, and so on.

- If the mother has complications and must stay in the hospital longer than usual, decisions about the services will have to be made. Be available to help in the home and give some respite to the husband, who will have many responsibilities at this time.

Make the Home an Easier Place to Be

- Some parents would rather put all the new baby items away themselves. Others may want a friend to do it. Ask.

- Laundry will pile up; do it.

- Groceries will be needed; get them.

- Ask simple questions without making judgments, especially where sensitive issues such as burial arrangements, guests after the service, notification of friends, etc., are concerned. Your questions may help the couple organize their thoughts for the difficult days ahead. If they are not ready to discuss such things, or prefer to have others take care of them, they will tell you soon enough.

- Most parents will be grateful if you remember their child—by name—on days that are significant (at one month, birthdays, etc.). Ask. Some couples prefer not to be reminded, or to keep these special times within the family setting.

The Environment of Grief

The environment in households with children, because of the constant concerns of daily life, tends to keep the parents' attention diverted from their sadness. These parents will most likely have *especially* bad days from time to time and feel incapable of rising above their grief. Friends can be "on guard" for these days and offer some special help. Possibly taking the other children overnight so the parents can have a few free hours to just let their emotions go or to get some extra sleep would be the right thing to do. Maybe it will be to push the parents out of the house so they can eat a meal alone, go to a movie, church—whatever. As a sensitive friend you will know *when* to offer, and the parents will know *what* they need most.

What to Expect When Your Friend's Child Is Disabled

If a newborn is disabled, there will be a series of endless tests to determine the extent of the disability. This is an emotionally exhausting time for parents. Hope mingles with depression, fear, and an overwhelming sense of inadequacy about what may be required of them.

The birth of a child with a severe disability is life-altering and must be faced daily. All kinds of thoughts race through parents' minds at such times. Before answers come from physicians and professionals, the parents' thoughts may swing from "things will be fine" to extreme fantasies of needing to live with extensive hospital care, constant treatment, and a twenty-four-hour-a-day regimen of actively caring for an unresponsive child.

Since most of us would not have the courage to do what we must in life if we knew it all in advance, friends should try to understand what the parents are going through *without projecting things into the future*. The speculation that causes parents such agony at the beginning will not necessarily be their reality. Changes occur one day at a time.

How to Help Friends with a Disabled Infant

Become an informed participant:

- Talk to professionals about the prognosis for babies such as the one your friends have.
- Contact the parents of children with similar conditions and talk to them about what life is like under these circumstances.
- Ask if there are parents who are willing to assist your friends, if they should want that help in the future. Get names just in case.
- Ask if there are informal or sponsored parent groups. Where and how often do they meet?
- Find out which physicians the parents trust to treat their child.
- See if you can talk to the parents of an adult with the same problem, especially one who has suc-

ceeded in amazing the professionals by his or her progress. Also, find out why the parents think their child has done so well. What combination of factors was the most helpful?

- Try to determine what kind of extraordinary care this child will need. If there is any special training required for the care givers, see if you can take information about it to the parents. Are there other friends who would be willing to help by taking the training?

- Please read the material on parental rights and insights in Chapter 9 and encourage your friends to use it to develop attitudes and coping methods that will promote healthy living skills.

Slaying the Dragon of Isolation

Some of the above suggestions make friendship seem like too much trouble. It is! That's not the point. As a friend, you determine the level of your involvement and how much of your time and caring can be committed to a serious situation such as the birth of a disabled child. If you are one of a group of friends, maybe you can organize the group so the commitment can be shared among all of you. Maybe your friend is a church member and some other members will get involved. Maybe the couple comes from a large family and you will not be called on for assistance, but your love for your friend will need to be shown, regardless. Friends can help a family by giving them extra strength to face the challenges ahead. Isolation will be the dragon your friends will have to slay in their new and strange venture.

Friends work magic by making aloneness disappear, even if it's just for a brief time.

When you are learning about the baby's disability, however, it's important not to force your information on the parents. When they're ready—in a few days, weeks, or months—you can be a great help to them during their time of transition. Everything you learn will offer the potential to support your friends and allow involvement with their child.

A well-known aspect of having a newborn in the home is sleep deprivation. If the infant has a disability requiring extraordinary physical care, the parents' sleep will be disrupted even further. During some of your free time—or not-so-free time—you could help by allowing your friends time to sleep while you look after the infant. Chances are you will not be able to convince them to leave the child with you in your home, but help at their home would probably be most welcome.

When parents have the least amount of energy, younger children sense it. They tend to be more demanding and become overactive. When a friend, Jennifer, had to spend time in the hospital caring for her second child, who was ill for many weeks, her husband and young daughter would visit. On one such visit, the daughter had what Jennifer called "a nervous breakdown in the hospital bathroom." She screamed that Mommy no longer loved her because she wouldn't come home. Jennifer said that aside from her mother, no friends offered to help with her daughter. Help, in this case, would have meant something as simple as a dinner, cartoon video, bath, story, and return home at bedtime.

An offer to take older siblings to your house for dinner

could also save the day. What a relief for new parents to have a break! What a special treat for the child (or children) as well, since they are more likely to behave better with attention focused on them in a setting away from the consuming crisis at home.

Friendship: a Steady Force

Most important is that we remain "tight" with the family during the first crucial weeks of their crisis. As time goes on, they will have more coping skills than they ever imagined possible. But in the initial stages they will need the moral support of people who know and love them. It's always upsetting to hear of people who spend a great deal of time with friends only to disappear during their time of misfortune. Harriet Schiff wrote that "people are basically decent," and I agree. Friends will truly want to help, but they will need guidance as well as the encouragement to be honest about how much they can handle. As Schiff says, and as this book demonstrates in specifying the complexities of various caring situations, "they need to be shown how." In showing your friends how, you may need to tell them that even if they are too afraid to help in this situation, you will understand and want to keep them as your friends, regardless. Taking the pressure off friends (who may be too embarrassed or ashamed to say anything about their fears) will allow them to understand that your feelings for them go beyond the physical conditions that have appeared to overshadow everything.

CHAPTER 12

❧❀❧

Living with AIDS

We have much more to offer than we may realize. All we have to do is ask, "How can I help?" with an open heart, and then really listen.

—RAM DASS AND PAUL GORMAN,
How Can I Help?

What can you do when a friend is diagnosed with HIV or has AIDS? Instead of feeling helpless or useless, you can give hope to your friend by being there for him or her. If that sounds too simple to be effective, please keep in mind that it's the single *most* important thing you can do. Don't avoid your friend. "More than anything," Magic Johnson said after finding out he had HIV, "I just needed to feel like I was still my normal self."

"Illness is the night-side of life," Susan Sontag once wrote. It is a potentially oppressive and lonely life-style for any afflicted person. Yet although any kind of illness brings the threat of isolation with it, ignorance and fear have made HIV and AIDS an especially lonely and burdensome experience for many. This is another case where friendship takes on a sacred dimension. You can bring light into the darkness. You can be a positive force by showing you care.

Do not let your friend become isolated. Though your friend may not initially be receptive to your calls or visits, he or she will eventually be grateful for your caring persistence.

Be the friend you have always been. You don't have to be glib or pretend that everything's okay. Try not to resort to lines such as, "You're going to be fine." Even in the early stages of your friend's illness, such easy (for you) assurances are rarely helpful. It's better to listen and try to be honest about how you feel. Be open and patient with your friend.

Let your friend cry if she or he wants to. As a friend, you can be instrumental in helping that happen. Your caring presence and advice will supply the strength to overcome whatever obstacles and difficulties you face with your afflicted friend.

HIV and even AIDS are not immediate death sentences. Your friend can grow in ways she or he may never have thought possible. So be aware that you may still have time to share intimate experiences, laughter, and tears.

Milton Mayeroff wrote, "In helping the other grow I do not impose my own direction; rather, I allow the direction of the other's growth to guide what I do, to help determine how I am to respond and what is relevant to such response."

In caring for your friend, remember not to be too hard on yourself, for as Mayeroff also pointed out, "Caring is compatible with a certain amount of blundering and lapse in interest and sensitivity to the other's needs." Patience during times of stress must also "include tolerance of a certain amount of confusion and floundering." Your patience, however, will express your belief in the continued well-being and growth of your friend.

That growth may take the form of wanting to be part of something larger than the self. Indeed, another way to help a friend with HIV or AIDS is to suggest the benefits of involvement in political advocacy or AIDS advocacy. This is a way to get your friend to know he or she is not alone. In a moving essay,* Robert Rafsky wrote that it was vital to him, even as he knew he was in a later stage of AIDS and was dying, to "Keep fighting the epidemic, and those whose actions or inactions prolong it, until I get too sick to fight."

You can be helpful by taking a moment to learn about support groups and other services. These services will be glad to suggest things you can do to help yourself help a friend in the education, research, and politics of HIV and AIDS. Start by suggesting a few ideas. Help with making a plan. Go with him or her to meetings.

Neal Hitchens, who is involved with AIDS Project Los Angeles as a volunteer in the AIDS wards of various Southern California hospitals, has said that most of all, people with AIDS want someone who will listen to them. "Maybe they can't talk to a loved one or a family member, but a person who is there can be a sounding board for their fears about the disease." Hitchens's comments speak to the central premise of this book: Friendship is more crucial today than ever before. Traditional family life—that illusory "haven in a heartless world"—has weakened itself by

---

* "A Better Life for Having Acted Up," *The New York Times* (April 19, 1992).

being intolerant, especially toward those who are "different."

"Rejection," said Magic Johnson, "is one of the worst things about having the infection. Discrimination is ugly. It's based on hate and ignorance."

Thank God for friendship! This force for good is growing as more and more people create new families out of their long-term friendships. The ties of friendship can be deeper than family ones, because we choose the relationships. The bond of friendship is as central to life as the air we breathe.

If your friend becomes seriously ill, you can help:

- Bring over a favorite food.
- Ask for a shopping list and deliver the goods.
- Bake cookies, bring over books or taped music.
- Suggest an outing, within the physical limitations of your friend.
- Help with the children, if any (make their lunch, dinner; take them to necessary appointments).
- Offer to help answer letters, phone calls, and write out and mail bills.
- Offer to water plants, feed and walk pets, do laundry.
- Ask about the illness—you will know when to change the subject to something else.
- Be tolerant and flexible about good and bad days.
- Acknowledge your friend's feelings if he or she implies concern for his or her looks. Talk about "cosmetic magic" that might work.
- Keep humor as part of your visits and conversations.
- Just keep your friend company. Listen to music or

read or don't do anything. Silent times can be very special.

- Don't be afraid to be part of conversations that include anger and frustration. Your feelings need not be suppressed because of the situation.
- Respect your feelings and the feelings of others who are caring for persons with AIDS. Support each other. This is heavy-duty, and it is easy to burn out if you don't take time to keep your balance.

Support for those who care for friends with AIDS is very important. They need to be able to get away from their duties, act silly if they want, and vent their feelings about their difficult situation. People who care for AIDS patients are the first line of defense for them. Those who support the care givers are the second line of defense, because they help the care givers to take care of themselves and maintain their equilibrium during stressful times. Because there are so many people stricken with AIDS, many care givers are friends with more than one friend who is ill, and they tend to become involved with the care of several people. Their work is heroic. Lastly, those in the gay community who are HIV-free are not without concern. They may feel guilt or gratitude about their health, but they cannot look at their sick peers without a particular sadness. Friends can be helpful by listening to them with empathy and allowing them to express their feelings freely.

Perhaps the biggest change in the way that HIV and AIDS are spreading is the absolute decrease in cases of AIDS among homosexuals. Each day 125 people die of AIDS in the United States alone. The most recent AIDS conference projected that worldwide by the year

2000 there will be more women than men with AIDS. This is already the case in some African countries. Lack of proper medical treatment and preventive education in many underdeveloped countries gives little hope that this disease will soon be under control. A recent afternoon TV talk show discussed women and AIDS and repeated this theme: "No woman is safe from AIDS." By the end of the show I'm sure all the viewers believed it. It is not difficult to understand that prostitutes are infecting many men, who in turn infect their wives. The wives may not even think about protection because they may be unaware of their spouse's infidelity. Many teenagers, ever confident that nothing bad is going to happen to them, refuse to take the threat of AIDS seriously. The homosexual community, whose ranks have already been decimated by deaths from this disease, seems to be taking it seriously enough to protect themselves and change their sexual behavior. One can only hope that those who believe God is punishing homosexuals by allowing this AIDS epidemic will wake up to the medical realities. Magic Johnson put it more succinctly:

> Many people have been taught that homosexuality is a sin . . . if that has been your upbringing, remember that the very same religious teachings also tell us that we are all sinners and are obligated to give the same loving attention to others that we would want for ourselves. . . . I am asking you to give your kids a sense that we are all God's creatures and that we all deserve love and compassion.

This manuscript was almost complete when I began a program of heavy-duty volunteering for people with AIDS, a plan opposed by some of my friends. "Too grim, too soon after your wife's death . . . and you haven't worked through your own grief." Contrary to their admonitions, I feel energized by the experience because I feel useful. We talk about the need to bear witness and to be supportive of each other. We have in-depth discussions about survivors' guilt and the meaning of life.

I recall one occasion when a young man talked about sadness to a group of couples. In each of these pairs, one was either HIV-positive or had AIDS. No, he didn't want anyone to relieve—let alone take away—his sadness. On the contrary, he revealed how he used his sadness to assess his priorities and to work out what was important to his life. Another time there was a discussion about whom to tell about one's HIV status. Even if one were not discriminated against, there was the terrible experience of being treated, unconsciously and sometimes even sympathetically, as a disease instead of a person. Personhood is often a casualty in the face of catastrophe.

In her book *Landscape Without Gravity*, Barbara Ascher tells about people who ask if she was close to the brother she lost to AIDS. Ascher writes, "I want to say, no, we were not close and that is why I grieve. This is the worst of all pains, the knowledge that it is too late to remedy failed love."

CHAPTER 13

❧❀❧

Facing Terminal Illness

When the diagnosis of a terminal illness is made, most people will maintain their medical treatment in the hope of a cure. Some will move in the direction of a road less traveled and seek alternative medicine, including what might turn out to be healthy doses of denial, with good results. Only when the physician says he can no longer do anything for the patient will some families pursue ways to make their remaining days together as full and painless as possible. Others will continue the "fight." It is a fine line. Often physicians are reluctant to admit they will not be able to effect a cure or even a remission of the disease.

Let me recount a personal episode. When Judith, my wife of thirty-eight years, fell ill with terminal cancer, it was a devastating time. Our many friends called to express sympathy, assured us we were in their prayers, flowers arrived in abundance, and a great many cards were delivered. Once we had "adjusted" (you can't, really) to what was happening and to what was required of us, we believed she was going to beat all the odds.

As weeks and then months went on, my wife showed

some improvement. The excellent medical and nursing care, chemotherapy, our own decision to use acupuncture (for pain and nausea relief), loving attention, and her own determination were having an impact on her health status. We held on to the hope of a remission (actually until the last month of her life), and this hope worked for us. We expected a miracle but didn't count on it. In any case, for the most part, our days were good. Periods of depression, hopelessness, and fear were confined to our intimate times together. It wasn't denial but a choice to live fully and with as much life and hope as possible. I think even those who have no hope for recovery might treat their illness in the same way. Regardless, each and every one of us can live only one day at a time—whether we choose to see life that way or not!

While we were dealing with new day-to-day routines, including endless medical treatments that had become our first priority, I began to respond differently to the people who asked if they could do anything. (There were things friends could do, but I was not able to say exactly what. I wasn't sure myself and I didn't feel I could ask.) I determined that my best responses were, "If *you* can think of something please do it" or "Surprise me." Some of our friends just faded away—somehow they were unable to react to our change of circumstance. Almost all of our very close friends did exactly the right thing. Those in close proximity made frequent, brief visits to the hospital and then to our home. They were concerned about me, the care giver. They frequently brought food and stayed in regular contact. We would and could call on them for anything (rides, household tasks, errands—anything). Our faraway friends quickly ascertained what we could handle in telephone conversations. They wrote letters and sent books and various entertainments. They did not expect return calls or thank-you notes. While I was worrying about life-and-death issues, the last thing I wanted to do was the "polite" thing—although sometimes I did. So my first bit of advice for helping a friend in a serious crisis is: *Make your presence known—carve out a task.*

If you live far away, determine how frequently your calls will be welcome. Write letters. We keenly wanted to be aware of how our friends were doing, and we wanted to feel that we were still part of their lives.

If you live nearby, prepare food and be available for comfort and listening. Suggest outings, even plan them, although a change in energy or feelings may prohibit participation. We always wanted to go, but sometimes Judith just didn't have the energy on the day of the event. Happily, most people understood and were not hurt or angry when, at the last minute, we couldn't go. When we could go on these excursions to the movies, out to dinner or a drive to the coast, we always enjoyed the company and the different surroundings.

Be an Informed Friend

Friends who think that another opinion, special treatment, or particular specialist should be brought in should do all the research first, find out if what they are suggesting is appropriate in similar cases, and then ask the ill person if he or she wants to hear about it. Don't just dump the question of another treatment in the person's lap. If you just mention that you heard about this or that treatment and then expect the family to respond and do their own research, you can forget it most of the time. They usually don't have the time or energy to challenge the status quo. This is a very touchy area because it confronts and questions the professionals and treatments that are being used, as well as the ability of the family to choose the correct treatment. If you feel strongly enough about a physician's work or a new combination of medicines, then do the work necessary to allow the family to understand that it is absolutely worth their time and energy. On the other hand, if you are knowledgeable about what they are doing for treatment and believe it is the right thing, tell them and encourage them—a little extra confidence in this area is an absolute help.

Friends will always remember and appreciate that you stood by them in a difficult situation. You didn't distance yourself, for whatever reason. No matter what happened, you were there. Be very careful not to overdo your concern for the care giver during a period of acute illness. It may make the person feel guilty and begin to think that he or she is not doing enough. Care givers don't want to be fussed over, at least not more than the person who is the object of concern.

A Difficult Situation: A Friend's Condition Deteriorates

Your friend has a terminal illness and is not long for this world. You know it, but she doesn't. You have both kept up the hope that some miracle will happen. You know that hope works. Already she has lived a year longer than the doctor's earlier prognostication of six months to live. But now she is deteriorating rapidly. In recent weeks she has been in and out of the hospital, and blood transfusions are becoming increasingly necessary. You can't handle it. Do you keep up the optimistic chatter? Yes, for as long as your friend wants you to. Suppose one day she says to you, "I'm going to die." You can't handle what you know is the reality of the situation. It seems so hopeless, and both of you have been using hope as the mainstay of every change that has happened during the course of her illness. You feel you can't watch her die now. You are so sad that you don't want to visit her with the same regularity that you have in the past. You have to! You are her best friend. Think hard. What would you want her to do if you were in her place? Visualize your own dying. It will help you overcome your fears and anxiety. Let your friend take the lead. Does she want to give you "instructions" about her funeral, about things she wants done after her death? Does she want to pretend and spend the time with you as though she is not dying? (That's okay too!) It's cruel not to allow her her last wishes. Unfortunately, some dying or extremely sick people become quarrelsome and very difficult (which may be associated with drug therapy, the disease itself, or mental deterioration). This is just something you will have to accept to the extent possible and not respond in kind but with kindness. "I'm sorry, I don't mean to hurt you." "Tell me what you would like me to do and I'll do the best I can." Assume your friendship is so strong that you will be able to do what will make her the most comfortable and that she will be honest with you and guide you toward that goal. Trust the best aspects of your relationship to carry you through. Difficult occasions, when faced squarely, often become the starting places for greater understanding and depth in relationships.

Living While Judith Was Dying

I am compelled to interject another personal note. When a spouse dies, it is very hard, but when that spouse was your best friend, it is even harder. My wife, Judith, was my best friend. As a witness, living with cancer was bearable for both of us when we had hope for a remission. There were lively periods when we could laugh and go for walks and watch *Jeopardy* together. We lived fully and did everything we could to prolong life, however difficult for us and painful for her. We embraced life. When Judith was dying we were both grateful that no one pushed us to prolong that process. Judith's life is a source of inspiration for me. Part of my adjustment to life without her has been to become an activist in the movement to respect the right of people to die with dignity. We learned something about dying, and it is my charge to help inform others about how they can maintain control over this most important life event.

Another process that helped us get past her illness to the point of enjoying life and hoping for the best is the fact that soon after her diagnosis we "took care of business." By that I mean we drew up our wills, made burial arrangements, sorted out papers, made lists of whom to inform, who should get particular household items, the location of all important documents, and many other details surrounding the change from "life as usual" to "life as it is." This was sad at times, but when the process was completed we both felt better. We had discussed how we felt about everything, from graves to the smallest household items that held special meaning to us and who should have them as heartfelt mementos of our caring. This work was not done because we had lost hope. On the contrary, when it was completed we devoted our days to our hope for a cure and the necessary treatments toward this end. Taking care of the business of death and closure freed us to spend our time together more fully, more honestly.

Illness Makes You Feel Inferior

I used to be big on the slogan, "Nobody can make you feel inferior without your consent." I still believe it to be true, but there are exceptional situations. Being gravely ill is one of those situations. Often people who are very sick feel inferior, and sometimes those around them inadvertently encourage these feelings of inferiority by making decisions for them or in other ways ignoring their personal integrity, which is not affected by illness except in extreme circumstances. Instead, provide some relief from the terrible feeling of helplessness. Be sure to speak directly to your friend, not *about* him or her to a spouse, nurse, or anyone who might be present. Also, don't assume you need to interpret how your friend is feeling. If or when this becomes necessary, you will know it. Help with personal care as much as is wanted and needed—within your comfort level. In exceptional circumstances you may have to provide it beyond your comfort level.

The Hospice Alternative in Care for the Dying

Hospice is specialized care. It emphasizes the management of symptoms, pain relief, and supportive services for those with a terminal illness. Ideally the care is given at home, where the patient and family are more comfortable and can control their own lives, although short-term hospital or nursing home care is possible. Medical care is coordinated by physicians but stresses a team approach, including nursing, counseling, and the assistance of homemakers and trained volunteers for the benefit of the entire family. Hospice programs operate on the principle that the patient should be as symptom-free as possible to use his or her energies for living. Since pain can be physical, psychological, spiritual, or social, they are all considered and treated. The latest pharmacological knowledge is used to keep the patient as pain-free as possible but still alert. Within hospice care there can be minimal to extensive care, depending on the variable needs of the patient and family. Although this form of care will not be chosen by everyone, just knowing that it is available will help. (The section on Resources will help you find a hospice in your community.)

The hospice movement has been growing in the United States for the past thirty years. When the prognosis is made that there is no hope for a recovery and less than a year to live, a person may opt for hospice care. Many insurance companies offer reimbursment for hospice care. Medicare, Part A, includes a hospice benefit for the terminally ill. *The Medicare Handbook* outlines the services, and the Social Security Administration will send this handbook to you upon request (there is no charge).

If you are a friend of a terminally ill person, you can find out what is available in your community. If you contact a hospice, you will be able to learn about the program on an informal basis before suggesting that the patient and family talk about this alternative with their physician. If a hospice is not part of the health care system where you live, you can still learn about hospice care and talk to your friend about setting up a variation of this care on an informal basis. A physician sympathetic to the particular problems of the terminally ill is the most crucial factor in making this kind of care work in communities where no licensed hospice exists.

Even in Dying There Is a Special Kind of Living

It is possible to find life in dying. Christine Saxton, feminist, teacher, and filmmaker, died of cancer at age forty-six. Before she died she wrote in her journal, "A safe place to die is a safe place to live. Will I find, if I go, that those I love will be there in that safe place with me after all? When you are holding on, how to let go! And who after all, do I really love."* The concept of a "safe place" takes on such a special meaning during the time before a death. It is more the people than the surroundings that provide the "safe place." By their love and attending to the needs and desires of the dying person, the participants form a symbolic protective circle around their friend, and it is felt

* As quoted in an article about how her support group of friends helped her while she was dying and themselves after her death. *San Francisco Examiner* (January 5, 1992).

to be a safe area. Living through this experience is profound, some would say sacred. One friend of mine likes to draw the analogy of illness and death as being like labor and birth. To her, the labor is difficult, uninspired work that somehow needs to be done, much like a time of a terminal illness (though certainly not often allowed in the same time frames). Birth, the most natural thing, somehow becomes supernatural, as does death. I'm not sure I believe as she does, but some elements of her analogy may make living through a terminal illness seem a bit more bearable.

When a death occurs, even if there was great openness between friends and family, there can still be some unfinished business in the relationships. Those who have been close tend to put some superhuman qualities on the experience. That is well and good unless "the goodness" of the death is exaggerated into an idealized situation that denies the humanity (frailties) of all those involved. Realistically there will always be something we forgot to say or finish up —that's human—we do it in life, and we do it unto death. We also make mistakes. Not all our actions were perfect, and not all the actions of the person who died were "saintlike." To say otherwise is a disservice to *life*. People "goof" and people forgive. No matter what really happened, we must admit that we all operate with imperfections. They're built in. Sometimes we feel regret, guilt, and sorrow for ourselves. Maybe we feel more human than humane. What is important, though, is that our feelings were and are authentic. Such authentic feelings can inspire us to become better persons. Our thoughts and actions often give us "clues" about genuine feelings. Do we become disorganized or inspired to change? We honor ourselves and our loved ones who have died when we understand and *accept* our own and their real-life frailties.

After the acute or initial stages of grief, many feel the need for the support of people in similar situations. Support groups for survivors have been instrumental in helping people, not with recovery as much as the courage to forge ahead with their lives in productive ways.

In interviewing people who have facilitated such groups, one common grievance expressed by most participants is the silence of their friends. Among friends, there is a lack of candor or even willingness to mention, let alone talk about, death. People who mourn are often (though certainly not always) ready to talk, to share memories and reflections on the meaning of life and the importance this person had on the lives of the people who are still alive. Talk about the deceased. You will find out quickly whether it is appreciated. Do not assume that a friend wants to mourn alone. Few mourners want privacy for very long. Most want and need contact.

PART III

~~✿~~

When Caring Is Most Challenging

CHAPTER 14

❧✿❧

Support for a Grieving Friend

Sarah and Tom's son Brian was killed by a drunk driver on his graduation night. He was a wonderful boy, on his way to Harvard. The headline in the local paper read, "An American Tragedy." Sarah and Tom mourned longer and deeper than their friends could handle. The grieving parents lost some of their friends in the process.

Within their own family, tension mounted because Sarah and Tom mourned differently from each other. The three surviving children also mourned in their own unique ways. Each individual needed a different, helpful response in order to derive some relief from tragedy.

Don't believe any of the stuff you read concerning "stages" of grief. Every death has a life of its own. An accidental death, a suicide, a prolonged dying from AIDS, an eighty-five-year-old mother dying peacefully in her sleep, a stillbirth—all of these events elicit quite different responses from family and friends.

Not everybody mourns hard, long, and tragically. That does not necessarily mean that they will suffer more later. Some people, because of their philosophy or religion, can "manage" grief—not better than but differently from others. I know of many situations where a husband and wife who shared the same grief responded differently. Sarah mourned at home, while her husband was able to return to work after a short time. Ten years later the family is a loving, cohesive, dynamically functional unit. Their son Brian remains a part of their lives, and they are all part of mine.

In some families the wife derives comfort from the fact that her husband is "strong" and can hold the family together. In many families the wife may feel the husband is not grieving enough, and the strain can be so devastating that the family breaks up.

Do Something for a Grieving Friend

It's true that traditional Catholic and Jewish practices, among others, can be enormously helpful and soothing by providing the framework within which grieving can be openly supported and not denied. Though these religious practices continue, fewer and fewer people choose to grieve within such familiar structures. It's no wonder that more people are responding to tragedy—which is an unavoidable and integral part of life and living—by doing little or nothing, or by saying they don't know what to say or do.

One of the most distressing thoughts that has emerged from interviewing hundreds of people for this book is that almost everyone recalled times when they regretted not having done the right thing to help a friend in trouble. Especially in cases where there was a death or a tragic occurrence in the family of a friend, people told me, "I should have gone over," "I should have called," and "I should have maintained my relationship." I heard these regrets so often that they became painful to record. These were not bad, uncaring, or mean people. In fact, most of us can probably recall similar incidents in our own lives.

Most recently, a good friend of mine lost two sons, one to suicide and the other to a medical tragedy. I knew both these young adult sons, but when the tragedies occurred I couldn't bring myself to make even a simple phone call (this particular friend lived three thousand miles away). I barely managed to write a coherent note. A week later, I forced myself to call. Maybe my own recent experience in dealing with the death of my wife was creating a barrier to being able to make contact with my friend. Yet I knew it was a block that had to be overcome. I knew it was the right thing to do, and as it turned out, it was.

You Can Support a Grieving Friend

If you can, be there! If you live far away, try to come to the funeral and stay (not necessarily at the house, unless you're invited and can be useful). If you live too far away, call regularly. Don't be discouraged if someone answers and says your friend can't come to the phone. Leave a message. Don't *expect* to be called back. When my wife died, I couldn't bring myself to make or return calls, or even to answer the phone for more than a very few people. Some of my friends wrongly interpreted this to mean that I wasn't interested in speaking to them. Some were sensitive enough to leave messages telling me it wasn't necessary to call back. They called again after some time had passed. At that time I was able to thank them for their understanding and talk about our loss.

If you are present, it isn't necessary for you to carry on a conversation. Just be there. Embraces, hugs, and crying together help.

Please don't say, "Call me if there is anything I can do." *Just do it!* Write notes or letters. *Good friends should not send printed sympathy cards*, which are appropriate only for acquaintances and business associates. No matter what you say to a grieving friend, it will be well received if you use your own words—even if they are few and awkward. Send or prepare food. I received a food package from a wonderful friend two months after my wife died. The box was filled with treats and snacks. It was very comforting to know that she and her husband were thinking about me. The thoughtfulness was much more important than the contents of the box.

Be sure you know if flowers are appropriate. They aren't at Jewish funerals. I'm sure other cultures and religions have traditions that are different from what we usually perceive as American. Be sensitive to those who have suffered the loss. Send plants or arrange for the planting of a tree. If you plan a memorial gift, please give to the charity designated by the family, rather than your own favorite.

"It's God's will" is often resented as an explanation for a death, especially when someone dies under tragic, meaningless circumstances. Most families will not be comforted by this response. Coming to terms with such deaths is much more complex than these words suggest, regardless of a family's commitment to their religion. "You are in my prayers," should be assumed if you are religious. That soothes, calms, and is helpful to some people. If you don't know what to say, simply say, "I'm sorry."

Please don't resort to inappropriate clichés such as these:

- "Time heals." (It doesn't. What heals is getting functional again, or back to work, or dedicating your life to a related cause such as gun control or MADD.)
- "You have other children to take care of."
- "It's time to get on with your life."

It's presumptuous and unhelpful when someone tries to be a hero in a friend's situation. Such selfish comments may make you feel better, but you can be certain they won't help the recipient—the grieving friend.

Staying Connected: A Personal Experience with Grief

There are many things you can do for friends over time. Staying connected to them is most important. That's what I wanted from my friends. I felt lost when my wife died. My anchor was gone. I appreciated it most when my friends called on a regular basis and kept me informed about their lives. I expected them to tell me about their good and bad times. They didn't push me to do anything, but expressed their pleasure when, after a couple of months, I started to do something (such as beginning this book). They understood when I told them things don't get better with time—only different.

Some of my friends—fortunately not my closest—

pushed me to get away from home and my routines; I resented such advice. Although this might be good for some people, I preferred to be home, alone with all my memories. Somehow these friends were *sure* that things such as sleeping in the same bed would be depressing for me. Not so. It gave comfort. I wanted to be alone and depressed. I resisted friends visiting. When I was ready, I wanted friends to visit, and I also wanted to get away and travel to see relatives.

I Missed Judith So

On January 1, 1992, I cried most of the day. I walked a bit, feeling terribly alone and lonely. I missed Judith so. I wasn't into denial; in fact when she died, I was relieved, because of the terrible pain she experienced during the last weeks of her life. Her dying was the most painful experience of my life, and yet the last thing I wanted (and I knew she felt the same) was to prolong her dying.

A couple of weeks before her death, Judith was ready to give up. It was enough, she said. I begged her to stay alive despite her excruciating mental and physical pain. My request was for selfish reasons. I wanted her to wait for her sister (who lives in England) and our son (who lived across the country), who were coming for a week's visit. She agreed and saw me through the sadness of what we knew was our last time together.

I don't know if I asked too much of her or if I did the right thing, but I did it. One day shortly after Judith's death I cried and had crazy thoughts and felt cheated. My whole existence seemed challenged. And that day, New

Year's Day, nobody called. I felt very sorry for myself and cried some more. Then I remembered that I'd been getting dozens of calls and I hadn't answered any of the hundreds of condolence letters and cards I'd received. I decided I still couldn't answer them. But I would try to write a little, especially after I recalled a poem I once wrote on a lonely Hanukkah day when Judith was in Israel for several weeks visiting her ailing, elderly parents. This is the poem.

Alone

feeling sorry for
the plants
unwatered
like my love
in the Fall of
life

I

seek the sun
among withered flowers
and brief encounters
where friendship lingers
not for long.
I am loved
not enough to still the
Exile. I lit two candles to

Find

The way. No one noticed
What is a way to a
Jewish holiday?
Then

God

responded, somewhat impatiently

I thought,
"For Heaven's Sake, Water The
Plants, And Get On With It."

I could not have realized how pertinent it would be to my situation during Hanukkah 1991 when, alone again, I lit the candles recalling the many years Judith and I shared this ritual with each other.

I didn't like it at all when some friends pushed me to go to a support group, though it can be a really good idea for some people. Again, "timing" is everything, and no one can prescribe the right time for someone else. I *hated* it when people said that in time I'd feel better and marry again, suggesting that it was not good for me to be alone. That may be so, but I can't imagine myself wanting to marry again, regardless of the circumstances. It was also totally irrelevant and hurtful for me to consider such things. Obviously many people do, which is fine for them. Bless sensitive friends who provide good company—without an agenda for your life.

I didn't make a big thing of the funeral. In the Jewish tradition, burial is usually within twenty-four hours of the death. A few of my good friends flew in for the funeral, but my wife had specifically asked that neither of her sisters, who lived abroad, should come. She had said her good-byes, and so I respected her wishes.

My friends and our son stayed with me for a couple of days. Then I wanted to be alone, and they respected this desire. Other people want and need company. The whole idea is for a friend to be sensitive to a specific individual's needs and wishes.

I believe an authentic friendship is like being in love

with someone who will be your partner, hopefully for life. It requires that you, more often than not, consider *his* or *her* needs as just a bit more important than having your own needs met. Do you agree? If you don't agree, then you might want to ask yourself if you have difficulty keeping friends.

Trusted Friends and Grief

Perhaps this would be a good time to mention that degrees of friendship are not measured by who does what task. Your love for your friend is best shown when you do what you do best—regardless of the attention paid to your efforts. If you have a particular talent with children, you can make sure they are given special attention and the opportunity to talk about their loss.

If you are a good organizer, be the person who mobilizes others to prepare meals for the family. In the context of a crisis, friendships take on serious responsibilities. It is a privilege to be among those entrusted to help during this profound time. If you feel yourself becoming jealous of another friend for the position he or she seems to have, feel the feeling, but keep it to yourself, or at least away from the mourning family.

Widowed and Left Alone

It's important to realize that people who have built their lives completely around their spouses may be in for a shock when a tragedy occurs. If you are just a "couple," then be prepared for the possibility of having no friends at all. My sister's case is actually quite common. When her husband died she was given a few weeks or so of the perfunctory condolences, the "Call me if you need anything," etc. Then, nothing. She lost all her friends a short time after her husband died at age forty-eight. Her whole society and culture were based on couples. There was no room for a single woman. When my sister heard that I was writing this book, she said, "Put in a plug for the singles. Tell their couple friends that, sure, we appreciate your coming to the funeral, your kind words, and invitations to go out—your treat. But, after that, include the widows and widowers in your activities and allow them to split the bill. We 'singles' feel more comfortable when we are paying our own way."

Children Grieve Too

Children who have lost a parent or a sibling can be devastated when they find that their own friends won't come around or won't allow the grieving person to talk about the death. You'd think that schools would include appropriate responses to death in their family-life courses. Some do, but most don't. Our culture seems not to prepare us to support and relieve grieving persons. As a society we deny the existence of death as a natural part of life, and nowhere is this denial more evident than in the way we try to shield children from it.

Although it seems obvious, children need special attention during times of intense grief. Their grief is often ignored by their friends, and adults may do the same thing without realizing it. Friends who visit after a death in a family will focus on the adults in the household, assuming the children are getting attention from their parents and other family members. Although this may be true—and we certainly hope so—it is up to the visitor to acknowledge the grief of the youngsters and spend at least some small amount of time giving them comfort, even if there are no words at all. Quietly holding hands in a corner of the room can say volumes to a child. The adult activity during condolence visits, followed by few if any guests, can be confusing for a child. Consider what they might need, and see if there is some way that you or a child of yours could structure some special, supportive activity. Children's and teenagers' grief is dramatically different from that of adults. Children and teenagers do not have the same consciousness or life experience that might give them clues about what is happening and how this death is going to alter their lives. Please don't forget the needs of the children, and if you have children, please teach them how to be empathetic friends rather than "*self*-conscious because they didn't know what to do."

When a Pet Dies

Some people respond to the death of a pet, especially dogs and cats, with intense grief. This should never be trivialized by comments such as, "You can always get another one." A good friend will always be supportive and offer to be with the person by going for walks and providing companionship. You don't have to say much.

You Don't Know How It Feels

In any case, *never* say to a grieving person, "I know how you feel." You don't. Even a best friend doesn't know. You can only sense the suffering, you feel only your own pain. It's impossible to truly experience another person's tragedy. Even years after a grievous loss of someone close, people report that it's like having a missing limb: There is a void, something is always missing in their lives. "One simply learns to tolerate more pain," an active professional person once told me, "and yet I have not wallowed in self-pity."

A friend was kind enough to write about her grief over the loss of her son some five years ago. She included a passage from Judith Viorst's book *Necessary Losses*, which she was reading to help her through yet another period of difficulty. Viorst knows that some losses are absolutely unforgettable, and so they should they be! Here is the passage:

> Perhaps the only choice we have is to choose what to do with our dead: To die when they die. To live crippled. Or to forge, out of pain and memory, new adaptations. Through mourning we acknowledge that pain, feel that pain, live past it. Through mourning we let the dead go and take them in. Through mourning we come to accept the difficult changes that loss must bring—and then we begin to come to the end of mourning.

Your grieving friend will probably not want to forget his or her loss. Indeed, many grieving persons appreciate it when their friends don't forget anniversaries, birthdays, and holidays that keep the memory of their loved one alive. That doesn't mean they are dysfunctional or that there is anything wrong with them. They are not fixated at a "stage" they should have gotten over.

When we recall the good influences that our loved one had on our lives, we actually honor them by remembering and acting in accordance with the best qualities they taught us. Two things facilitate getting on with one's life. One is maintaining a sense of humor. The other is recognizing that there is hope. It's hard to imagine that this is so because the circumstance of mourning is grim. Even though friends need to allow for the grimness, they also need to find appropriate times for laughter and a sense that things will become better.

The Language of Hope

The semantics of grief is important. Those in mourning must be able to express their loss in ways that are meaningful to them. Friends need to listen, but they also need to express their own feelings about the loss. Each person differs in the way he or she talks of the person who died and the length of time it takes before the emotions and subsequently the words change. "My life is over" must eventually give way to "That part of my life is over." The language of hope becomes important. Again, it is not a matter of forgetting, but an ongoing process that accepts the loss and incorporates it into what is today and what is anticipated for tomorrow.

When Grief Alienates Friends

We must also acknowledge that sometimes the grieving person creates a situation that alienates friends. At a dinner party several years ago, I met a woman who had lost her husband two years earlier. Even during this first meeting, she had little to say about anything except the "sanctity" of her late husband and her own constant suffering. The hostess, who was the best friend of the woman, later apologized for her friend's behavior. She said that everyone she knew was weary of the widow's constant "whining," but they all felt obliged to include her in their activities.

In such a situation, where a friend is stuck in a dead past and is letting self-pity rule his or her present, the responsibility of a best friend is clear. The troubled friend must be told about the effect such behavior is having on those who want to be supportive.

If you ever find yourself in a similar situation, it is always better to confront your friend and risk losing the friendship. After a certain length of time, self-pity becomes boring, even to the mourner. The person in my example clearly needed to learn how to mask her sorrow in public, for her own sake as well as that of her friends.

I'm also reminded of an experience I once had on a national talk show. The topic was "How to Help When Someone Is Lonely and Miserable." Also on the panel were four of the most pathetic people I had ever encountered. Each had a tale of woe that seemed unending! After listening to all this wretchedness, I was asked what I would do to help. Much to the distress of the program's hostess, I responded that I would find it difficult to be around these people, much less be their friend. Who would want to be around such incessantly gloomy people?

It took the rest of the show to redeem myself with the hostess. Obviously she had expected me to be empathetic and gentle, but I found nothing to indicate that the self-indulgent people on that panel wanted help. The best response for needy people like these is to tell them, "If you want to make friends, 'you have to fake it until you make it.'" It's an old AA slogan, but it's just as relevant for people wallowing in self-pity. If somebody asks how you are, for example, answer, "I'm okay," regardless of how you feel.

The panel discussion also brought home another point: The slowly emerging, still adjusting, and lonely person should not tell everyone about his or her sadness. It's best to reserve it for close friends.

In the end, the best way to get out of the funk, or trap, of selfhood is to do good deeds for others, which is exactly what I suggested to the talk show panelists. The idea of doing good deeds is as old as the Bible, though it's becoming known lately as "helper's high." I have always called it "mitzvah therapy." The ability to do mitzvahs is a crucial component of any good, long-lasting friendship. (It's also one of the best ways to start a friendship.) Helping each other, while expecting nothing in return, is one of those marvelous paradoxes in life. By caring for another person, we help ourselves in deeply satisfying and lasting ways.

CHAPTER 15

❦

Responding to an Overwhelmed Friend

An article in *The New York Times* (January 1, 1992) described a support group for relatives taking care of people with Alzheimer's disease. What struck me immediately was an observation concerning one of the members of the group: "Like many other care givers, Mrs. Nagel said she had lost a lot of friends since undertaking the care of her father."

For reasons I couldn't explain, I started to cry. Alone in my study, I shouted out to nobody, but really to the whole world, "Why the hell should you have lost a single friend?" Mrs. Nagel's tragedy should have meant the strengthening of bonds with all her friends. Yet the plain fact is that most of the fifty or more people I spoke to while writing this book who were also caring for adults with disabling conditions lost *most*, and in some cases all, of their friends within a year's time.

Under certain circumstances, such as taking care of a relative with Alzheimer's disease, support groups can be extremely helpful. Through them we become acquainted with others in a position similar to ours. The isolation, tedium, and emotional strain of being a care giver is given a forum within these groups. We can profit from each individual's experience and share others' knowledge of the available community resources. Such associations often generate needed strength and courage to their members, a welcome by-product of group dynamics. The commonality of experience may also lead to new friendships.

Staying Sane: Relaxing and Recharging

During our trips abroad, my wife and I often made it a point to converse with older adults who appeared to be traveling alone. The story of one woman was especially enlightening. She told us about her husband, who was an Alzheimer's patient. She had been his care giver for ten years because she felt it was her duty, and would not consider any other role for herself. But she did do one thing for herself: Once a year she would take a three- to four-week vacation on her own, arranging with one of her children to care for the father while she was gone. Looking forward to this special time, this break from her responsibilities, kept her from going out of her mind.

Although this woman devoted most of her days to staying home with her husband, we soon discovered that her life force was strong. She was a lively, outgoing companion and easily made new friends. She said she kept in touch with the people she met on vacation during the eleven months she was home caring for her husband. They became an important part of her support group even though her "visits" with them were by phone or through letters. I can't stress too much or too often that relief and respite are needed to maintain the energy and *attitude* necessary to care for someone who is ill.

A Brief Note on My Role as Care Giver

As I said earlier, my wife, who was ill for a year and a half, felt well enough most of the time to talk, have visitors, and participate in the daily activities around the house. I did enjoy, without guilt, the times when her good friends would stay with her, either at home or when she was in the hospital. During those periods I would take a walk, meet with a friend or associate, or enjoy a leisurely meal. Not only were these times refreshing for me, but my wife also enjoyed hearing about my activities because they introduced some different "news" into our conversations, which, as you can imagine, might have become focused only on her illness rather than on living each day as it came.

Homebound Care Givers

Being homebound when you are well yourself but the primary steward of another is probably one of the worst parts of care-giving. Your life is literally given over to the other. In many ways, *both* the care giver and the sick person are victims of the illness. Although most care givers would not change their situation—other than having their loved one well again—this does not mean that they would not welcome some diversion and stimulating activities that have nothing to do with illness. Being a friend to the care giver might mean that you spend whatever time and energy you have to give your friend in any of the following ways—or better ones, as you think of them.

- Stay with the infirm person while the care giver goes to a support group, church or synagogue, or movie.
- Enlist the care giver in projects that can be done at home (toymaking, crafts, cooking, writing or stuffing envelopes, repair of household items for resale, etc.) for a church, synagogue, or other charity, or for yourselves if money is an issue. Work together when possible. If working for a charity, see if some other members can go to the care giver's house to work on the project at convenient intervals.
- See if the care giver would like to "barter chores" with you and others: a batch of cookies for you in exchange for grocery shopping or mowing the lawn, or start bedding plants from seed in return for some of the plants from his or her yard. (The ideas for this type of activity will be limited only by your combined imaginations about how together you can improve your quality of life through this kind of sharing.)
- Discussion or study groups would be great. Groups that discuss best-sellers or classic literature are very educational and stimulating. Movie critiques would also be easy, with VCRs and rentals available. (You all agree to read a certain book and come together to discuss the work. The care giver might want to host the group often, in which case others would bring refreshments. Maybe the wife, husband, son,

or daughter of the host would sit with the infirm person while the care giver is at the study group.)

- If there is a neighborhood program of any kind (such as providing a safe house for children walking home from school or calling a certain number of homebound persons to ensure that they are okay), find out about it and see if the care giver could help that group.

- If the care giver enjoys children, and her charge is not terribly demanding, she may want to provide after-school care for a working mother or two. The child can get homework done and possibly help with some chores. The relationship would be helpful to all concerned.

When the Care Giver's Well-Being Is Threatened: Steps toward Outside Help

There are situations where families must consider day care or nursing home care for their relative. I, for one, feel this is often necessary and desirable. I'm very sad when people tell me of the guilt they have about such placements. To the relentless pressures of their care giver role, they have now added guilt, making matters worse for everyone concerned. Some care givers even allow themselves to become dysfunctional. What is the point of this punishment? It certainly doesn't help anyone in the situation.

Only rarely do families make such decisions when other options are still open to them. A complex set of circumstances leads to such decisions. No outsider can understand the family dynamics well enough to judge (nor should they,

in any case) the actions of the family members. This is not
to say that a decision is not extremely complex and guilt-
ridden. Two friends of mine, who are a homosexual couple
of long standing, were confronted with a decision about
how to help the elderly mother of one of them who was no
longer able to live by herself. Fully realizing that it would
be an extraordinary "burden" to both of them, they decided to arrange the spare room for the mother and take all
necessary steps for her care in their home. But an odd
thing happened at about the same time. Two of their good
friends, a heterosexual couple, distanced themselves and
would not offer any explanation for their sudden coolness.
My friends couldn't figure out what could have created the
breakdown of their relationship. Some months later they
discovered that their friends were forced to make a similar
decision, and theirs was to arrange for nursing home care
for one of their parents. It turned out that they felt so
guilty about this decision that they couldn't face being
confronted almost daily with their friends taking the opposite position, however much my friends were totally sympathetic with the others' decision. (Obviously, whether the
couples were homosexual or heterosexual has nothing to
do with the situation aside from the fact that I decided to
keep it a true story.) Again, I am not about to be a hero in
somebody else's situation, and I have to admit that sometimes the decision to place someone in a nursing home
seems like the best possible decision. Conversely, I can't
help thinking about an old Jewish saying, "A Jewish
mother seems to be able to take care of five children, but
five adult children seem to have difficulty taking care of
one Jewish mother." One must also keep in mind that
there are, in virtually every community, organizations and

voluntary groups that are geared to help homebound elderly and infirm people stay independent. It could be the responsibility of a friend to find out about these resources.

If you are a friend to someone who has had to place a relative in a nursing home, you could offer to visit once in a while. If you think such places are depressing, even when they offer pleasant surroundings and excellent care, think about how your friend feels. If he or she must work all week and has a family to care for, the hour or two you spend visiting will mean some precious personal time for your friend. Short visits are relatively easy to do, yet they mean more than these few lines on the subject can express. You need do it only once to understand what I mean.

Caring for the Care Giver: After the Death of Their Loved One

One last but very important insight for friends to know about: Often people who were longtime care givers and who revealed remarkable strength, resiliency, and resistance to illness will, on the death of their loved one, become lethargic, prone to illness, and seem barely able to manage any aspect of their own life. We should not be surprised by this response to the end of a consuming interest, to say nothing about the loss of a love. This is the time for a *friend* to care for the care giver. Don't push the person to "get well." After a while (and this helped me), the best advice from a friend was: "Look, don't even try to get back to normal. Just make an effort to accomplish one simple thing during the day. It doesn't matter what it is. Make a call, pay a bill, keep your dental appointment, get a haircut

—and I'll help if you want me to." Don't have any time-tables for the healing process of your friend. One good week or month does not necessarily mean that the process will continue in such a forward direction. Feelings, energy, and determination to "carry on" will ebb and flow for no apparent "reason." Maintain your support without any agenda for the other. Keep a positive approach, but remember that complex interactions are going on that can confuse your friend as much as they confuse you. If you have expectations for "what should happen next," forget them. Life isn't that orderly, and certainly someone who is learning a totally new life-style without their loved one will have many "fits and starts" before getting any speed or direction.

In your effort to help someone, please go back and read the section on "being stuck." Some of the suggestions will help you decide what you can do to help and encourage your friend.

❧✿❧

Getting "Better"

Still, there's no denying that in some sense I "feel better" and with that comes at once a sort of shame, and a feeling that one is under a sort of obligation to cherish and prolong one's unhappiness.

—C. S. Lewis, *A Grief Observed*

There are so many elements in the world and within our bodies, feelings, perceptions, and consciousness that are wholesome, refreshing, and healing. If we block ourselves, if we stay in the prison of our sorrow, we will not be in touch with healing elements.

—Thich Nhat Hanh, *Peace Is Every Step*

As you have probably noticed, many of my personal experiences in dealing with grief and other matters may have solid points of identification for you or your troubled friend. That's good! I'd hate to think that my thoughts and feelings during my own personal crisis were so unusual as to be unrelated to the experiences of others. With that in mind, let me share a few of my observations now, two years since my wife's death. This part is also for people who have lost their own best friend.

I found that even the darkest grief can change for the better. While writing this book, I learned that you *do* get better. So, believe me, your *friend* will get better too.

I began to feel better when the images of my wife appeared before me more frequently as vibrant and alive than as dead and dying. When a loved one has suffered a long illness or dies after an accident, our last images of them may be so powerful as to temporarily overwhelm, or even blot out, the good things about their life and the joys of their relationship to us. This is temporary. Now I find the good, happy, and wonderful feelings are reemerging. I often find myself wondering what she would do when I must make a decision. Her counsel is present. With such a long marriage between us, we discussed everything *at least* once. I know what her words would be, and they are consoling . . . her advice is as sound as ever.

I also began to feel better when I could sometimes enjoy myself without feeling guilty. After my wife's death, my usual routines, habits, and even passions appalled me.

So I found myself living in two worlds. In the public world, I appeared to be feeling better; but in the private one, I was feeling worse. That began to change, however, when the wide gulf between my private and my public self slowly began to narrow.

I realize now that when people asked me what they could do, it shifted the responsibility away from themselves and onto me. I knew I didn't want that responsibility.

In the initial stages of my grief, what seemed to upset me the most was the failure of many friends and relatives to even mention the death of Judith when we got together. Somehow they never picked up the signal that I *wanted* to talk about her. I wanted them to share part of their grief, which I knew they felt. Unless I initiated the conversation, however, mention of Judith was rare.

My sister-in-law revealed a distress very similar to mine. Within a month, she lost both her son and her sister. Did I say "lost"? That's a strange word, because neither of us felt we had lost them. They were still, and would always be, ever present for us. We both wanted to recapture our memories and all the experiences we had shared together and with friends.

Yet I started to feel better when I was no longer bothered about how friends and relatives responded to Judith's death. If I wanted to bring it up, I did, and people responded appropriately. I hope the message, however, is clear. Don't hesitate to at least acknowledge your own feelings. It will be very obvious to you if the person most affected by a death will want to discuss it further.

I also began to feel better when my crazy thoughts became less frequent. Thoughts of dying myself, of earthquakes and other disasters, and of the possible deaths of everybody else I loved preoccupied me. For several months I lived as if I were going to die imminently. Now, past seventy, I am living as though I have many more years of life. That attitude shift makes a big difference. The notion of living one day at a time is dumb. It's appropriate only when you are really dying. In any case, you can't make plans that way. I have plans, and they involve things I want to do years from now. As Scott Nearing once said, "You don't get old when you have plans."

Another thing that made me feel better—not well, but better—was when I truly accepted the fact that one cannot in a sense share suffering. Suffering is individual. It's a state of being with its own integrity, and the intensity of it varies from hour to hour and from day to day. Yet in another sense we do "share" suffering, when we reveal our pain at times of readiness to friends. The burdens of suffering can be reduced by the loving care of friends and relatives. That is the best that can be expected.

To help grieving friends, keep these observations in mind so you can allow their grief to be as it is while you gently offer the support that will help them find the healing directions their lives could eventually take.

In helping a grieving friend, as in all areas of true caring, we must try to experience the other person as an individual in his or her own right. When we fail to do this, even if we are doing a lot of other helpful things, we are not truly caring for that person.

For grieving people to be "comfortable," they need to incorporate their loss into daily life. This does not mean "letting go," "forgetting," or waiting around for time to heal. Instead, comfort comes when the grieving person is able to appreciate his or her life *as it was* while beginning to blend it into the one that is evolving *now*.

The world of a grieving friend is a special one. For a time it may appear closed to you. Hang in there! A crisis is no time to be dropping or losing friends, so please *don't* mind your own business when a friend is in trouble!

Keep in mind that no one can take responsibility for anybody else's sorrow. As a friend or relative, you can be

there for comfort and help. To assist a grieving person effectively and to maintain a clearer understanding of what
may be going on, however, we must never assume that we
are experiencing the same feelings as our grieving friend.

Most important is for all of us to realize that there *is* life
after great pain. When we assist a friend in finding that life
and then help him or her to make the most of it, we create
another, potentially deeper and more enduring stage of a
friendship.

In truth, two years have passed, but I still don't know
how to live my life. I'm living it anyway. I travel. See
friends. Go to the movies. I'm writing and reading again. I
have learned that suffering is not ennobling and that,
somehow, one must find a way to live again. That may take
a while, perhaps years, but that's the obligation of people
who are still alive.

One thing I *do* know: To have friends, you need to be
one. For me, nothing in life seems worthwhile without
them.

Please remember . . .

When someone you care about is very sad, especially as
the result of a disabling illness or a recent tragedy, helping
him or her cope with feelings of isolation and despair is the
most important role you can have. And perhaps you will
make this promise to yourself: If you receive sad news from
a friend, you will make every effort to respond fully to that
friend, at the "moment" of crisis, and not so much to your
own distress. And will you remember *not* to say, "I know
how you feel"? A full bear hug might be the most desirable
initial response.

Now ask yourself these questions:

- Will I be a friend when my friends need me?
- Can I count on my friends when I need them?
- Is there a better time than now to pay attention to the friendships in your life?

❧

Helping a Friend Find Assistance from Community Groups

Whether it is for yourself or a friend, there will be times when you need to know about particular helping groups or agencies within your community. Without social service experience, finding these organizations and groups who assist with services may feel like a major mystery. Rather than a mystery, finding the right help can be like going through a maze. The puzzle becomes very simple if the solution is sought by taking the right steps. The first and most important step is to use the telephone and telephone book to their best advantage.

For the sake of this example, let's suppose you have a good friend who was recently diagnosed with lupus. You know nothing about lupus (an autoimmune disease in which individuals develop antibodies to their own nucleic acids and cell structure, causing many of the body's organs and joints to dysfunction), and your friend needs your support. She is distraught and cannot think beyond how this disease is going to change her life. You give her your empathy, but you know you need to learn *how* to help. Your time is limited, so you want to go directly to the source of the most information.

With pad and pencil ready, look in the white pages of the phone book under "Lupus." Most not-for-profit organizations do *not* use Yellow Pages advertising. Since the Lupus Foundation of America is a large organization, they have a national office with an 800 number as well as local chapters. Especially if you live in a small community, the 800 number will allow you to make an initial contact and have information sent. They will be able to tell you the location of the closest local chapter. Local chapters of the Lupus Foundation meet regularly. You will want to speak directly with one of the members to find out if they have someone who volunteers for the organization who can help you understand more about what they do at the local level and how the organization can support your friend through her illness.

There are so many organizations to help individuals with social and medical problems, crisis situations, and emergency assistance that sometimes it is difficult to know whom to call upon. I hope the following explanation will help you learn how to discover the best and most useful organizations in your community. For those living in rural areas, the process may require more mail than direct contact, especially if the organization you need is not large enough to put a listing in every telephone book or if they do not have enough money to subscribe to the 800 telephone network. In any case, your friend will appreciate your concern and your good deeds in her time of need.

Getting Through the Resource Maze

Use the white pages of the telephone book first.

1. Look up the name of the organization you think might help—AA, Al-Anon, Arthritis Foundation, Lupus Foundation, Muscular Dystrophy Association, Nar-Anon, etc. (If you don't know the name of any organization in your community that helps with your particular concern, see number 2, below.)

2. Look under "Information and referral" or "Helpline" in the yellow pages. These lines may be manned only during business hours, or they may be twenty-four-hour-a-day, seven-day-a-week services; communities differ.

3. If you do not find either of these references, look under "United Way" or "Volunteer Center." (Information and referral services and/or helplines are often operated by these organizations.)

4. You can also look in the government pages. (Start with "City," then "County," then "State," and sometimes the "Community Resource" pages in the front of the white pages.) Within these government categories are the departments that handle particular social problems (e.g., "Mayor's Office," "Social Services," "Health Department"). Under these departments look for headings such as "Child Abuse Council" or "Adult Protective Services." You have to look for the department name that seems most logical, although there is no guarantee that your thinking and the government's will

mesh. Regardless, once you call, most personnel will assist you in finding the right office or person.

5. Try "Crisis" (again, in the white pages) if you think there may be a *crisis line* in your community dedicated to helping the particular problem you are trying to educate yourself about. Sometimes these organizations will list their service in several places to make finding them easier (e.g., "Crisis Pregnancy Center, The," and "Pregnancy Crisis Center").

6. After exhausting these direct services to no avail, call a local hospital and ask to speak to its Social Services Department. The amount of knowledge they have will vary greatly from community to community, but it is always worth a try.

7. If none of these resources is available in your community, look in the Yellow Pages under "Churches." Don't worry about denomination unless your own mind-set tells you not to call certain ones. Some churches list the work they do for the community. If they have a food bank, sponsor AA meetings, etc., they will name them along with their address and service hours. Many times the pastors and rabbis belong to an ecumenical organization and know quite a lot about what each church and synagogue is doing (this helps them to not duplicate their social service programs).

8. Please do *not* call 911 for information. If you have a crisis situation and need instant advice, call the police station nearest your neighborhood. They can help.

With pencil and paper ready, write down all the information you can. Organize your paper so you will be able to read and remember what you found out by phone, so when you want to act on the information it will be easy to go back to. It will help if you set up a page to write down all the information you need. A format similar to this may help:

ORGANIZATION   PERSONS   NOTES   PHONE NUMBER

If you are very fortunate you will get all the information you need with one or two phone calls. But it is more likely that you will make more contacts than that and that the information you get will be cumulative, becoming more directed and specific with each person you talk to. Be prepared to be put on hold several times. I like to spend a minute preparing myself to be patient on the phone. You might need to use these folks more than once!

Have a list of questions ready. Here are some examples:

1. What services are offered?
2. Are there regular meetings?
   a. When?
   b. Where?
   c. Is there a contact person?
   d. Is public transportation convenient, or is parking available?
3. Are there support groups?
4. Are there clinic hours?
5. Is there a resource person who visits or can give

detailed answers to more specific questions about
_____? (Name the problem.)

   a. How do I contact this person? (Get the name
     and phone number.)

6. Do you know of other organizations that assist
with this problem? (Get their names and numbers
and run your questions by them as well.)

7. Do you have an information packet you can mail
to me?

8. Is there a reading list or specific books you recommend?

9. Is there a charge for services? Will insurance
cover them? If not, is there a sliding-scale fee
schedule?

10. Are there other organizations nearby that offer
similar services? Are they not-for-profit or for-
profit? (Call them all.)

As you make contacts about a particular problem you
will become familiar with the names of the most active
people in the field. Be sure to contact these people for
further information, or continue to ask for the most helpful
person you come across by name as you make subsequent
calls. Their consideration of your situation will become
personal and will be invaluable to you as time goes on.

GENERAL RESOURCES

Getting Some Balance on "Self-Help"

Auw, André, Ph.D. *Gentle Roads to Survival . . . Making Self-Healing Choices in Difficult Circumstances.* Boulder Creek, Calif.: Aslan Publishing, 1991.

Kaminer, Wendy. *I'm Dysfunctional, You're Dysfunctional.* Reading, Mass.: Addison-Wesley, 1992.

Mental Illness and Depression

NAMI
2101 Wilson Blvd., Suite 302
Arlington, VA 22201
(703) 524-7600
(703) 524-9094 (fax)

Klein, Donald F., M.D., and Paul H., Wender, M.D. *Understanding Depression: A Complete Guide to Its Diagnosis and Treatment.* New York: Oxford University Press, 1993. Focuses on the biological and organic factors.

For more information about depressive illness, write to:

Humanistic Mental Health Hotline (twenty-four-hour)
1-800-333-4444
Call them if you feel depressed or suicidal; their trained hotline staff can help with all types of problems.

National Depressive and Manic-Depressive Association
730 N. Franklin, Suite 501
Chicago, IL 60610
(312) 642-0049

National Foundation for Depressive Illness, Inc.
P.O. Box 2257
New York, NY 10116
(212) 268-4260
(212) 268-4434 (fax)
Or call:
National Mental Health Association
1-800-336-1114

For those who must cope with the daily reality of mental illness:

Dearth, Mona, et al. *Families Helping Families—Living with Schizophrenia*. New York: Avon Books, 1986.

Deveson, Anne. *Tell Me I'm Here—One Family's Experience of Schizophrenia*. New York: Penguin Books, 1991.

Fantle-Shimberg, Elaine. *Depression: What Families Should Know*. New York: Ballantine Books, 1991.

Lefley, H. P., Ph.D., and D. L. Johnson, Ph.D., eds. *Families as Allies in Treatment of the Mentally Ill: New Directions for Mental Health Professionals*. Washington, DC: American Psychiatric Press, 1990.

Styron, William. *Darkness Visible . . . Memoir of Madness*. New York: Vintage Books, 1990. A terrifying and brilliant account of the descent of one of America's preeminent writers into a painful depression. Anyone who wants some insight into depression will find this book compelling. Styron says, "I felt loss at every hand. The loss of self-esteem is a celebrated symptom, and my own sense of self had all but disappeared, along with any self-reliance. This loss can quickly degenerate into dependence, and from dependence into infantile dread. One dreads the loss of all things, all people close and dear. There is an acute fear of abandonment. Being alone in the house, even for a moment, caused me exquisite panic and trepidation." [pp. 56–57]

Torrey, E. Fuller, M.D. *Surviving Schizophrenia: A Family Manual.* New York: Harper & Row, 1988.

Homosexuality

The main thing is to learn as much as you can about homosexuality and homophobia. There are lots of books, but here are a few starters:

Bach, Gloria G. *Are You Still My Mother?* New York: Warner Books, 1985.

Fairchild, B., and N. Hayward. *Now That You Know: What Every Parent Should Know About Homosexuality.* New York: Harcourt Brace, 1979.

Hilton, Bruce. *Can Homophobia Be Cured?* Nashville, Tenn.: Abingdon Press, 1992. Raises the questions of what churches will do with the growing scientific evidence that same-sex orientation is neither an illness nor a matter of choice.

McNaught, Brian R. *A Disturbed Peace.* New York: St. Martin Press, 1990. The best introduction by one of America's most effective spokespersons for gay rights.

Monette, Paul. *Becoming a Man . . . Half a Life Story.* Orlando, Fla.: Harcourt Brace Jovanovich, 1992. A passionate, astonishingly candid, angry, and brilliant autobiography of a gay man coming to terms with coming out.

The following organization is designed to assist parents and friends who are not comfortable with their children's or friends' orientation or who need more information and/or support; its principal function is that of keeping families in loving relationships:

Federation of Parents and Friends of Lesbians and Gays, or Parents FLAG
Federation Office
P.O. Box 27605, Central Station
Washington, DC 20048-7605
(202) 638-4200 or (303) 321-2270

For Anyone Worried About Aging or Having a Midlife Crisis

Gerzon, Mark. *Coming into Our Own: Understanding the Adult Metamorphosis*. New York: Delacorte Press, 1992. "The mystery of the adult metamorphosis is that we now experience ourselves interconnected with something larger. We sense sacred oneness with all of creation. . . . We are being called home. We do not know by whom, or to where, but that, after all, is our quest."

Jarvik, Lissy. *Parent Care: A Compassionate, Common-Sense Guide for Children and Their Aging Parents*. New York: Bantam Books, 1990.

LeShan, Eda. *It's Better to Be Over the Hill Than Under It: Thoughts on Life over Sixty*. New York: Newmarket Press, 1990. "Old age is no excuse for copping out. Each of us can find ways in which to make a difference." A wonderfully warm and compassionate book; I loved reading it.

Nearing, Helen. *Loving and Leaving the Good Life*. Post Mills, Vt.: Chelsea Green, 1992.

A Gift for a Neurotic Friend

Ellis, Albert. *How to Stubbornly Refuse to Make Yourself Miserable About Anything—Yes, Anything*. New York: Lyle Stuart, 1988.

Ornstein, Robert, and David Sobel. *Healthy Pleasures*. Reading, Mass.: Addison-Wesley, 1989.

Abusive Men

Ending Men's Violence Task Group
c/o RAVEN
P.O. Box 24159
St. Louis, MO 63130
(314) 725-6137
Its referral directory lists programs for men nationwide.

Child Abuse

If you fear that someone you know is harming or will harm a child, contact:

> Child Help National Child Abuse Hotline
> 1-800-422-4453

> National Committee for Prevention of Child Abuse
> P.O. Box 94283
> Chicago, IL 60690
> Publications on parenting and child abuse and other subjects are offered through the free catalog. Puts callers in touch with chapters in every state.
> (312) 663-3540

> Parents Anonymous
> 6733 South Sepulveda Blvd., Suite 270
> Los Angeles, CA 90045
> 1-800-421-0353

Domestic Violence

> The Domestic Violence Toll-Free Hotline
> c/o Michigan Coalition Against Domestic Violence
> P.O. Box 7032
> Huntington Woods, MI 48070
> 1-800-333-7233
> 1-800-873-6363—TDD number for the hearing-impaired, twenty-four hours a day. Provides information and referral to a support group or battered women's shelter anywhere in the United States.

Jones, Ann, and Susan Schechter. *When Love Goes Wrong*. New York: HarperCollins, 1992. A guide to freeing women from abuse, guilt, and blame. Detailed and pragmatic advice for women who are being abused.

Helping Parents with Difficult Adolescent and Adult Children

National Runaway Switchboard (twenty-four-hour)
1-800-621-4000
1-800-448-4663 or Hutch Home
Crisis intervention for runaways and their parents. Referrals for other problems.

Toughlove International
P.O. Box 1069
Doylestown, PA 18901

York, David and Phyllis. *Tough Love Solutions*. New York: Bantam Books, 1985.

Alcoholism and Drug Abuse

Alcoholism is big time. The front cover of *Modern Maturity* for February–March 1992 carried these headlines: "Under the Influence—11 Million Americans Are Hooked on Alcohol—76 Million Have an Alcoholic in Their Family." The lead article was written by Nan Robertson, author of *Getting Better: Inside Alcoholics Anonymous* (New York: Ballantine/Fawcett-Crest, 1988), an insightful critique of AA.

AA is probably the best program to consider for most alcoholics who are not too far gone, as well as for those who are "recovering." (Al-Anon and Alateen are for spouses, teenagers, and others whose lives are affected.) For those who are turned off by the religious (albeit nonsectarian) orientation of AA, the following resources should be considered:

Families Anonymous
P.O. Box 528
Van Nuys, CA 91408

Rational Recovery
P.O. Box 800
Lotus, CA 95651
(916) 621-4374 or (916) 621-2667

Rational Recovery Systems
Joe Gerstein
521 Mount Auburn St., Suite 200
Watertown, MA 02172
(617) 891-7574

Secular Organizations for Sobriety
P.O. Box 5
Buffalo, NY 14215-0005
(716) 834-2922

Christopher, James. *S.O.S. Sobriety*. Buffalo, N.Y.: Prometheus Books, 1992.

Trimpey, Jack. *The Small Book. A Revolutionary Alternative for Overcoming Alcohol and Drug Dependence.* New York: Delacorte, 1992.

Other resources and recommended books:

National Clearinghouse for Alcohol and Drug Information
P.O. Box 2345
Rockville, MD 20852

National Council on Alcoholism and Drug Dependence
12 W. 21st St.
New York, NY 10010

Barley, Joseph V. *The Serenity Principle: Finding Inner Peace in Recovery.* New York: HarperCollins, 1990.

Ellis, Albert, and Emmett Velten. *When AA Doesn't Work for You: Rational Steps to Quitting Alcohol.* Emeryville, Calif.: Barricade Books, 1992. Another brilliant Ellis (rational emotive) book, with no punches pulled.

Fossum, Merle H., and Marilyn J. Mason. *Facing Shame: Families in Recovery.* New York: W. W. Norton, 1986.

Kellogg, Terry, with Marvel Harrison. *Broken Toys, Broken Dreams: Understanding & Healing Boundaries, Codependence, Compulsion, and Family Relationships.* Amherst, Mass.: Brat, 1990.

Scales, Cynthia G. *Potato Chips for Breakfast: A True Story of Growing Up in an Alcholic Family*. New York: Bantam Books, 1986. A tell-it-like-it-is autobiography of a young girl struggling to survive in a family with two alcoholic parents.

Twerski, Abraham J. *Caution: "Kindness" Can Be Dangerous to the Alcoholic*. Englewood Cliffs, N.J.: Prentice-Hall, 1981.

Williams, Cecil, with Rebecca Laird. *No Hiding Place*. San Francisco: HarperCollins, 1992.

Planned Family Interventions

Bratten, M. *A Guide to Family Intervention*. Deerfield Beach, Fla.: Health Communications, 1987.

Johnson, Vernon. *I'll Quit Tomorrow*. New York: Harper & Row, 1980.

Johnson, Vernon. *Intervention: How to Help Someone Who Doesn't Want Help*. Minneapolis, Minn.: Johnson Institute, 1986.

Ketcham, K., and G. Gustafson. *Living on the Edge: A Guide to Intervention for Families with Drug and Alcohol Problems*. New York: Bantam Books, 1989.

Pinkham, Mary Ellen. *How to Stop the One You Love from Drinking*. New York: Putnam, 1986.

Disabilities and Chronic Illness

Dickman, Irving, with Sol Gordon. *One Miracle at a Time*. New York: Simon & Schuster, 1993. A paperback designed to answer the hundreds of questions parents have about raising a child with a handicap.

Felder, Leonard, Ph.D. *When a Loved One Is Ill: How to Take Better Care of Your Loved One, Your Family, and Yourself*. New York: New American Library, 1990. The author's personal experience caring for chronically ill loved ones helps to make this book authentic. As a therapist, Dr. Felder incorporates professional assistance as well. The survival of the family unit that is caring for a sick member will be greatly improved by using this book as a guide.

Register, Cheri. *Living with Chronic Illness: Days of Patience and Passion*. New York: Bantam Books, 1989.

Simons, Robin. *After the Tears: Parents Talk About Raising a Child with a Disability*. Orlando, Fla.: Harcourt Brace Jovanovich, 1987. "You can believe that your child's condition is a death blow to everything you've dreamed and worked toward until now. Or you can decide that you will continue to lead the life you'd planned and incorporate your child into it."

Coping with Miscarriage, Stillbirth, and Infant Death

Diamond, Dr. Kathleen. *Motherhood After Miscarriage*. Holbrook, Mass.: Bob Adams, 1991. Written by a doctor, this book offers the reader her personal experience with multiple miscarriages, plus the detailed medical information many women who have miscarried do not get from their personal physicians.

Ilse, Sherokee. *Empty Arms*. Maple Plain, Minn., Wintergreen Press, 1990. To help you accept, yet not forget.

Limbo, Rana K., and Sara Rich Wheeler. *When a Baby Dies*. La Crosse, Wisc. Resolve Through Sharing Press, 1990. A handbook for healing and helping.

Schiff, Harriet Sarnoff. *The Bereaved Parent*. New York: Penguin Books, 1977. Timeless help for parents who must face the loss of a child. Friends who are trying to support grieving parents will find this book both comprehensive and beneficial.

AIDS

Buckingham, Robert W. *Among Friends: Hospice Care for the Person with AIDS*. Buffalo, N.Y.: Prometheus Books, 1992.

Froman, Paul Kent. *After You Say Good-bye: When Someone You Love Dies of AIDS*. San Francisco: Chronicle Books, 1992. Excellent help for anyone dealing with death—AIDS-related or not. The wisdom of Dr. Froman is evident on every page. Direct and practical, with concern for all those involved—families, partners, care givers, and friends.

Goldstaub, Sylvia. *Unconditional Love: Mom! Dad! Love Me! Please!* Delray Beach, Fla.: Harbor City Publications, 1991. The life and death of publicist Mark Goldstaub of AIDS at age thirty-seven. A poignant story of rejection, despair, and eventual triumph of family acceptance and love.

Hitchens, Neal. *Fifty Things You Can Do About AIDS.* Los Angeles: Lowell House, 1992. Includes a directory of AIDS service and research organizations and safe sex guidelines.

Johnson, Earvin "Magic." *What You Can Do to Avoid AIDS.* New York: Times Books, 1992.

Sources of information:

Gay Men's Health Crisis
129 W. 20th St.
New York, NY 10011
(212) 807-6655

National AIDS Hotline
1-800-342-AIDS

National AIDS Information Clearinghouse
1-800-458-5231

National Leadership Coalition of AIDS
1150 17th St. N.W., Suite 202
Washington, DC 20036
(202) 429-0930

Death and Dying

Let's face it: For many people, the fear is about dying (painfully), not about death (which would be welcomed). The organization Choice in Dying (formerly Concern for Dying and The Society for the Right to Die) is committed to improving the conditions in which people spend the last days of their lives. They believe that individual choice about medical treatment should be honored—that no one should receive unwanted treatment, nor should commonly available treatment be withheld unless the patients or their spokespersons agree with that decision. While not now supporting legislation to legalize aid in dying, they did support the grand jury that decided not to prosecute Dr. Timothy Quill for prescribing barbiturates for a patient with leukemia, knowing that she intended to kill herself.

For more information, write to:

Choice in Dying
250 W. 57th St.
New York, NY 10107
(212) 246-6973

The Compassionate Friends
P.O. Box 3696
Oak Bridge, IL 60522

(312) 325-5010
For parents who have lost a child.

If you can't get information about hospice care in your locale, write to:

National Hospice Organization
1901 N. Moore St., Suite 901
Arlington, VA 22209
(703) 576-4928

Books on Death and Dying

Buckman, Dr. Robert. *I Don't Know What to Say: How to Help and Support Someone Who Is Dying.* New York: Vintage Books, 1992. A comprehensive aid for people who desire to help in the most suitable way. Compassionate and still realistic, this work directs and teaches with great sensitivity toward both the patients and their helpers.

Callahan, Maggie, and Patricia Kelly. *Final Gifts: Understanding the Special Awareness and Needs and Communications of the Dying.* New York: Simon & Schuster, 1992.

Gootman, Marilyn. *When a Friend Dies.* Minneapolis: Free Spirit, 1993. A much-needed, beautifully written book for children who are grieving the loss of a friend.

Humphry, Derek. *Final Exit*. New York: Dell, 1992. Makes explicit the subtitle of the book (originally published by the Hemlock Society in 1991): *The Practicalities of Self-Deliverance and Assisted Suicide for the Dying*.

Lamberton, Richard. *Care of the Dying*. London: Penguin Books, 1980. A realistic, down-to-earth book about caring for the dying within the context of hospice care. An invaluable resource for anyone who is taking care of a terminally ill person. Compassionate, but also states the case against euthanasia.

Rollin, Betty. *Last Wish*. New York: Warner Books, 1987. "I did not directly help my mother commit suicide," Rollin explained. "I did the research and gave my terminally ill mother the information she wanted."

Seibert, Dinah, M.S., Judy Drolet, Ph.D., and Joyce Fetro, Ph.D. *Are You Sad, Too?* Santa Cruz, Calif.: ETR Associates, 1993. Suggestions for teachers, parents and other care providers of children to age ten.

The Hemlock Society
P.O. Box 11830
Eugene, OR 97446
(503) 342-5748
The general principles of the Hemlock Society are:
1. Hemlock seeks to provide a climate of public opinion that is tolerant of the rights of people who are

terminally ill to end their own lives in a planned manner.

2. Hemlock does not encourage suicide for any primarily emotional, traumatic, or financial reasons in the absence of terminal illness. It approves of the work of those involved in suicide prevention.

3. The final decision to terminate life is ultimately one's own. Hemlock believes that this action, and most of all its timing, to be an extremely personal decision, wherever possible taken in concert with family, close friends, and personal physician.

4. Hemlock speaks only to those people who have sympathy with its goals. Views contrary to its own that are held by other religions and philosophies are respected.

Suicide

American Association of Suicidology
2459 S. Ash St.
Denver, CO 80222
(303) 692-0985

American Suicide Foundation
1045 Park Ave.
New York, NY 10028
1-800-531-4477
Referrals to survivor groups; information about their work and goals.

Bolton, Iris. *My Son . . . My Son: A Guide to Healing after Death, Loss, or Suicide*. Atlanta: Bolton Press,

1993. (For a copy, write to the publisher at 1325 Belmore Way, NE, Atlanta, GA 30350; the cost of $12.95 includes postage.) (404) 393-1173

Lukas, Christopher, and Henry M. Sieden. *Silent Grief: Living in the Wake of Suicide*. New York: Bantam Books, 1990.

Smolin, Ann and John Guinan. *Healing After Suicide of A Loved One*. New York: Fireside Books, 1993.

Vad Tikvah Foundation (a suicide prevention task force)
Union of American Hebrew Congregations
838 Fifth Ave.
New York, NY 10021
(212) 249-0100
A task force that is geared to American Jewry but open to all. Also publishes the illustrated version of *When Living Hurts* by Sol Gordon.

Cancer

A good source of information:

American Cancer Society, Inc.
Atlanta, GA 30322
See especially these pamphlets:
Questions and Answers About Pain Control
The Treatment of Pain in the Patient with Cancer

Life After Cancer
Cancervine

Bloch, Annette and Richard. *Guide for Cancer Support-ers*. Call the Bloch Foundation Cancer Hotline—(816) 932-8453—or write:
R. A. Bloch Cancer Foundation
4410 Main St.
Kansas City, MO 64111

Department of Health and Human Services
Public Health Service
National Cancer Institute
Bethesda, MD 20892
(301) 496-4000
Pamphlets:
Support for People with Cancer and the People Who Care About Them
Taking Time

Nessem, Susan, and Judith Ellis. *The Challenge of Life After Cancer*. Boston: Houghton Mifflin, 1991.

Grieving

The books I like the best are written by Earl H. Groll-man and include:

Talking About Death: A Dialogue Between Parent and Child, 1981
Time Remembered: A Journal for Survivors, 1987
What Helped Me When My Loved One Died, 1981
(All are published by Beacon Press, Boston, Mass.)

The book I'd send to a grieving adult after the initial shock or despair is lessened would be Earl Grollman's beautiful book of poetry *Living When a Loved One Has Died*, Boston, Mass.: Beacon Press, 1977.

The next book is especially good for religious people who find it difficult to face the religious implication of a tragedy: Kushner, Harold S. *When Bad Things Happen to Good People*. New York: Avon Books, 1981.

A similarly important work is: Lewis, C. S. *A Grief Observed*. San Francisco: Harper & Row, 1961. He writes, "It is hard to have patience with people who say, 'There is no death' or 'Death doesn't matter.' There is death and whatever is matters. And whatever happens has consequences. . . ."

Also beautifully written are:

Bullsman, Robert. *I Don't Know What to Say: How to Help and Support Someone Who Is Dying*. New York: Vintage Books, 1992. "Thoughts that a person tries to shut out will do harm eventually."

Cole, Diane. *After Great Pain: A New Life Emerges*. New York: Simon & Schuster, 1992. "Would we ever connect again? Would the death of my mother be the death of my family as well?" A superbly written memoir of pain, loss, and despair emerging into renewal, redefinition, and hope.

Collick, Elizabeth. *Through Grief: The Bereavement Journey*. London: Darton, Longman & Todd, 1986. "The very pain of grief has within itself the power to heal; it is the way, indeed it is the only way, by which the bereaved come to terms with their loss." Accepting death and the grief that follows is difficult in our "quick fix" society. Elizabeth Collick Darton helps us come to terms with this meaningful part of life.

Neeld, Elizabeth Harper, Ph.D. *Seven Choices: Taking the Steps to New Life After Losing Someone You Love.* New York: Delta Books, 1990. All the emotions felt by those who lose a loved one are opened for examination and acceptance by this sensitive author, whose husband died suddenly and without warning. She brings us with her during the journey of grief and allows us to feel and understand the worst of it as well as her road back to an integrated life. Anyone experiencing loss, either by death or divorce—be it parent, spouse, child, or friend—will appreciate the wisdom of this book.

Noll, Peter. *In The Face of Death.* New York: Viking Press, 1989. "Love those more who love you; devote yourself less to those who don't love you."

Schoeneck, Therese S. *Hope for Bereaved.* Syracuse, N.Y.: Hope for Bereaved, Inc., 1991. "What we once enjoyed we can never lose." A beautifully inspired book.

Silverman, Phyllis R. *Helping Women Cope with Grief.* Beverly Hills, Calif.: Sage Publications, 1981. Mourning must include a repair of the "spoiled identity" and the changes toward a new one.

Tatelbaum, Judy. *The Courage to Grieve: Creative Living, Recovery, and Growth Through Grief.* New York: Harper & Row, 1984. "If we are able to tolerate the intensity of grief feelings and to let go of our self-consciousness about doing the right things, there is much we can give the bereaved. Tolerating another's tears is a very meaningful gift. So is listening without judging."

Viorst, Judith. *Necessary Losses, a Gift of Hope: How We Survive Our Tragedies.* New York: Ballantine Books, 1986. "We idealize other people's relationships when in reality most people have unfinished business with the loss of a loved one."

Volkan, Vamik D., and Elizabeth Zintl. *Life After Loss —The Lessons of Grief.* New York: Scribners, 1993.

Death of a Spouse

Brothers, Joyce. *Widowed.* New York: Ballantine Books, 1990. "The pain is necessary . . . only by experiencing it to its full degree can you heal yourself."

Caine, Lynn. *Widow: The Personal Crises of a Widow in America.* New York: William Morrow, 1974. A poignant personal odyssey of one of the more than 15 million widows in the United States. "Our society is set up so that most women lose their identities when their husbands die. . . ." Still true and still one of the best books to help widows move ahead on a road forward.

Campbell, Scott, and Phyllis Silverman. *Widower: When Men Are Left Alone*. New York: Prentice Hall, 1987. "But part of living in this world is also a matter of searching after and finding ways of being connected." Includes a list of self-help organizations and readings.

Silverman, Phyllis. *Widow to Widow*. New York: Springer, 1986. Bereavement is seen as a process by which the widow is not cured of grief but is charged by it. It is about widows helping other widows.

Standacher, Carol. *Men and Grief*. Oakland, Calif.: New Harbinger, 1991. A guide for men surviving the death of a loved one. A resource for care givers and mental health professionals.

Comforting Books

Edelman, Marian Wright. *A Measure of Our Success— A Letter to My Children and Yours*. New York: Harper & Row, 1993.

Butterfly Kisses
Hummingbird Words
Roots and Wings
All are by Marvel Harrison and Terry Kellog and are available from Brat Publishing.

Pogrebin, Letty Cottin. *Among Friends*. New York: McGraw-Hill, 1987. "Friendship is a heart-flooding feeling that can happen to any two people who are caught up in the act of being themselves, together, and who like what they see. The feeling is deeper than companionship; one can hire a companion. It is more than affection; affection can be as false as a stage kiss. It is never one-sided. We know it when we feel it but we can spend several years trying to put it into words."

Affirmations for your spirit to soar, and notes to nurture by:

Buber, Martin. *The Way of Man: According to the Teaching of Hasidism*. New York: Citadel Press, 1950. "Every person born into this world represents something new, something that never existed before, something original and unique."

Frankl, Victor E. *Man's Search for Meaning*, rev. and updated ed. New York: Washington Square Press, 1984. "In view of the possibility of finding meaning in suffering, life's meaning is an unconditional one, at least potentially."

Gracián, Baltasar. *The Art of Worldly Wisdom*, trans. Christopher Maurer. New York: Doubleday, 1992. Three hundred beautifully crafted maxims covering many of life's situations. Those trying to do their best in this life will find this both instructive and comforting.

Mayeroff, Milton. *On Caring*. New York: Harper & Row, 1971. "In caring I experience the other as having potentialities and the need to grow. . . ."

Broyard, Anatole. *Intoxicated by My Illness and Other Writings on Life and Death*. New York: Clarkson Potter, 1992. When I was putting this book to bed with the notion that "finished already" means not another book or idea or thought is going to prevent me from saying I'm done—I've done the best I can, and every book has an "all done" clarion call—I didn't count on having *Intoxicated* thrust on me with such a tremendous impact on my soul. (In Yiddish I'd call it *kiskiz*, which Yiddishists will know has nothing whatever to do with soul or even solar plexus. Just take it to mean that I was blown away.)

New York Times book reviewer Broyard was literally intoxicated by his illness (terminal cancer of the prostate) and was filled with desire ". . . to live, to write, to do everything." He felt that desire itself gave him the immortality to carry on, however brief his term.

His friends rallied around him. "I can't help thinking there's something comical about my friends' behavior—all these witty men suddenly saying pious, inspirational things." They were sober and he refused the responsibility of being serious. "They appear abashed or chagrined in their sobriety. Stripped of their playfulness these pals of mine seem plainer, homelier—even older. It's as though they had all gone bald overnight." Broyard "spends" his time telling and listening to stories, being witty, playing with metaphors. Broyard says, "It may not be dying we fear so much, but the diminished self." Broyard wanted to make sure he was alive when he died. He felt that inside every patient was a poet who wanted to get out.

Friends of people who are struggling with their response to terminal illness should allow this book some play in their own encounters with illness. If every physician would read Broyard's prescriptions for humanizing illness, illnesses of all kinds would be transformed to a form of poetry (however sad, joyous, or bittersweet).

If I'm ever in a similar situation—slowly dying—I'd want all my friends to read Broyard's book before they came to visit me. Broyard says, "There comes a point where it's pretty obvious that a patient is going to die, and I think to eke out a few more days by mechanical means is a mistake, and I think the patient should be allowed to glide or skate or dance into death in the way that he chooses rather than be ministered to until the last minute, which I think is obscene. You know when a patient is moribund, and then you leave him alone. You let him die in his own way, and you let him make his final arrangements unimpeded by technology." [pp. 64–65]